Basic Pr...

Conservative

INVESTING

*9 principles
you must follow*

R I C H   B R O T T

Published by

ABC Book Publishing

AbcBookPublishing.com
Printed in U.S.A.

Basic Principles of Conservative Investing:
9 Principles You Must Know!

© Copyright 2007 by Richard A. Brott
10 Digit ISBN 1-60185-018-2
13 Digit ISBN (EAN): 978-1-60185-018-8

This publication is designed to provide interesting reading material and general information with regard to the subject matter covered. It is printed, distributed and sold with the understanding that neither the publisher nor the author is engaged in rendering religious, family, legal, accounting, investing, financial or other professional advice. If any such advice is required, the services of a competent professional person should be sought.

Every effort has been made to supply complete and accurate information. However, neither the publisher nor the author assumes any responsibility for its use, nor for any infringements of patents or other rights of third parties that would result.

ABOUT THE AUTHOR

Rich Brott holds a Bachelor of Science degree in Business and Economics and a Master of Business Administration.

Rich has served in an executive position of some very successful businesses. He has functioned on the board of directors for churches, businesses, and charities and served on advisory boards for colleges.

He has authored over twenty books including:

- *5 Simple Keys to Financial Freedom*
- *10 Life-Changing Attitudes That Will Make You a Financial Success*
- *15 Biblical Responsibilities Leading to Financial Wisdom*
- *30 Biblical Principles for Managing Your Money*
- *35 Keys to Financial Independence*
- *A Biblical Perspective On Tithing & Giving*
- *Basic Principles for Maximizing Your Personal Cash Flow*
- *Basic Principles of Conservative Investing*
- *Biblical Principles for Becoming Debt Free*
- *Biblical Principles for Building a Successful Business*
- *Biblical Principles for Financial Success – Student Workbook*
- *Biblical Principles for Financial Success – Teacher Workbook*
- *Biblical Principles for Personal Evangelism (out of print)*
- *Biblical Principles for Releasing Financial Provision*
- *Biblical Principles for Staying Out of Debt*
- *Biblical Principles for Success in Personal Finance*
- *Biblical Principles That Create Success Through Productivity*
- *Business, Occupations, Professions & Vocations in the Bible*
- *Family Finance Handbook*
- *Family Finance Student Workbook*
- *Family Finance Teacher Workbook*
- *Public Relations for the Local Church (out of print)*

He and his wife Karen, have been married for 35 years. Rich Brott resides in Portland, Oregon, with his wife, three children, son-in-law and granddaughter.

DEDICATION

This book is dedicated to:

- Those who comprehend the importance of sacrificing today, for benefit tomorrow.

- Those who believe in the wealth-building power of investments in an open, free, market-driven economic environment.

- Those who want to balance risk with reward.

- Those who understand that prosperity has a purpose.

- Those who are willing to study investment alternatives on their own instead of blindly taking investment advice from someone else who may or may not have their best interest in mind.

Specifically, this book is dedicated to the persons listed below who each understand the significance of the above commentary.

- My grandniece LaJoy Anthony, who according to Grandpa David, at just nine years of age, is a good saver and frugal buyer; she also understands the importance of sacrificing today, for benefit tomorrow.

- My former personal assistant Anna Jaquith, now a competent manager, who is well on her way to becoming a great investor.

- My nephew Andrew Brott, an experienced auditor and accountant, who has been managing his own investments for many years now.

TABLE OF CONTENTS

INTRODUCTION

Nothing ventured, nothing gained is an old axiom often quoted. While this is usually true whether you are thinking about starting or buying a business or simply investing what you have accumulated in other businesses, it can also be true that everything is ventured and nothing is gained. The latter provides much of the thought that has gone into this book.

After spending a lifetime (or even a short time) working hard, sacrificing and accumulating, nothing puts a damper on the spirits more than seeing it dwindle away in some equity position or high yielding bond that went south.

Good investing really is not rocket science, every though many salespersons (financial consultants, investment brokers, etc.) would like for you to think that it is much too complicated for you to do it apart from their advice (earned commission).

The book starts by encouraging you to set aside monies so that in time you have something to invest. The pre-investment process begins by being prepared for those unexpected emergencies. Following that you must be on a path to reach those short term and long term financial goals. With this out of the way, you can turn your thinking to retirement and your long term well-being. If you have already retired, it's all about preserving what you have and making sure that your money always outlasts you.

So get out a notepad, your pen and record some insights and "to do" lists as your read its contents.

To Successful Investing!
Rich Brott

Principle One

Finding the Money to Invest

I nvesting can be very complicated or very simple. It can be very successful or disastrous. There is risk with investing and there is risk in not investing. Investing can be very enjoyable or very distasteful.

In this book you will be given some overall and well-rounded investment information. Absolutely no attempt will be made to influence you to invest in a specific type of financial instrument.

We must first recognize the risks involved in all investments and what you can do to minimize those risks. So that you don't go down this path, common mistakes that lead to investment disaster will be reviewed. This will be followed by several principles you need to know about investing in mutual funds.

Next some alternatives for your investment consideration will be presented, with a discussion of their various advantages and disadvantages. After that the subject of retirement planning will be examined.

Spend what you have left after saving, instead of saving what is left after your spending.

Spend what you have left after saving, instead of saving what is left after your spending.

The purpose of this book is simply to give you enough information so that you can make your own wise financial investment decisions.

Before getting into the main content of the book, let's talk about finding the money to invest. Where does the infant investor find the money to invest? Here is a basic principle for you to follow. The secret of finding money to invest is to: spend what you have left after saving, instead of saving what is left after your spending.

Long-term investing is your best hedge against inflation, but you need to save in order to invest. This can be tough to do. Have you ever noticed that after you pay your monthly bills, buy groceries and cover your other expenses, you have little left in your paycheck? Consider contributing to your savings plan first, not last, each month.

A Three-Part Savings Strategy

Saving money is hard work. And the hardest part is simply getting started. If you're beginning from scratch, consider this three-part strategy:

➡ 1. Save for the unexpected: six to twelve month's worth of living expenses. In case you lose a job or find yourself with no steady income, this rainy-day fund will become necessary. Take no chances with this money. Keep it readily available, in a bank account or in a money-market mutual fund.

➡ 2. Save for long-range expenses: a new home or college for the kids. Be more flexible with this money. Keep it in long-term certificates of deposit or in U.S. Savings Bonds. You may earn more interest than in a conventional bank account and you can time your investment so the money is available when you need it.

➡ 3. Save for retirement: that can mean an Individual Retirement Account, a company retirement plan, or other solid financial investments. A conservative mutual fund that invests only in top-quality stocks is one possibility. Or you might risk a little more for a greater reward by investing in a mutual fund that buys growth stocks.

AUTOMATED SAVINGS

The following steps can help you make this practice automatic:

➤ Set up an automatic payroll deduction. Thanks to payroll deduction programs, such as credit unions or 401(k) plans, part of your paycheck can go directly into your investment account.

➤ Saving is easy: What you don't see, you won't spend.

➤ Set up an automatic bank transfer. Many investment companies will transfer money automatically from your bank account to your investment account according to a schedule that you specify. Such a program can make saving for retirement as natural as paying the mortgage.

➤ Invest all salary increases. Direct half of your next raise into an investment account before it reaches your wallet and before you get used to spending the extra income.

➤ Invest lump sum payments. Invest a portion of bonuses and tax refunds; you'll turn the extra money into added savings, not increased spending.

A FEW STARTER TIPS

Set Savings Goals

Start with 5-10 percent of every paycheck. It's easiest if your employer deducts it from your pay because you don't miss money you don't see.

You could also ask your bank to move it from checking to savings every month or make automatic investments into a no-load (no sales charge) mutual fund.

Saving is more certain when someone else arranges it for you. The goal may be college for the kids. It may be retirement in a few years. It could be a new car, a boat or a summer place.

A real key here is that it forces you to think ahead, beyond the next paycheck. Any successful business is one that plans for the future; many times, 5 and 10 years ahead. Many companies project plans even longer.

Pay Yourself First

After taking care of your charitable obligations, the next person in line to be paid is you. Although this seems very hard to do with all of our other obligations, just get started by forming a regular habit. It will get easier as you progress. Use direct deposit for automatic savings. It can be much easier to save when the money goes directly into a savings account. In that way, the decision to save is out of your hands. What you don't see, you are not likely to miss as much.

Avoid Spending on Impulse

Most of us save too little because we spend too much on impulse items. Control that urge to splurge. Keep a list of all the things you really need - coats for the kids, a new refrigerator, tires for the car, etc. But wait to buy until those items go on sale. If you're drawn to something not on the list, give yourself a week to think it over.

Save All Extra Money

Once you have paid off a loan, start paying yourself by putting an equivalent amount of money directly into savings. If you have a car loan you're about to pay off and you've been paying $250 a month, keep the car for a couple more years and save that $250 each month. Some people plan so there's a tax refund each year, but most financial planners suggest handling your taxes so you don't overpay. After all, Uncle Sam doesn't pay any interest on the overpayment.

17 Practical Ways to Save Your Money

1. Develop new habits.

Become a skillful shopper. Regional retail centers are exciting places. In supermarkets, thousands of goods line the shelves and invite attention. It takes skill and determination to pass down the aisles and resist temptation. The skillful shopper prepares a shopping list before going to market and buys only those items needed.

Learn to read labels and interpret them. Make substitutions for the higher priced items, judge the value of the week's bargain offerings and decide whether the best buys are best for the family. Careful shopping can save many dollars a week in the budget.

2. Get rid of credit card debt.

Here is a good way to save some big money fast. There is one great investment that is sure to pay off, yet we fail to recognize it, even though it's right in front of us every month. Pay off your credit cards! Let's say for example that you owe $2000 on a Visa card. Many charge cards still have an interest rate in the neighborhood of 19 percent.

Instead of taking that $2000 bonus check and investing it into some low-interest-paying bank account, pay off that credit card and get a great return on your money! By paying off the outstanding balance, it is the same as getting a check for $570 tax-free! And one more thing: be a real friend to yourself by cutting up the card and canceling your credit. You'll be glad you did! It's the best financial investment you can make.

If you're in the 30 percent state and federal tax bracket, paying off an 18 percent credit-card debt provides the same return as an investment that yields 26 percent! If you're in the 17 percent bracket, paying off credit cards is the same as earning 22 percent. Why keep money in a 5 percent (or less) savings account when it can earn 22 percent paying off your credit cards?

3. Use installment credit sparingly.

Recognize that any installment purchase or loan means one more fixed expense in the budget. Although credit is readily available and most anything can be obtained, be wary of the low-down, low-monthly-payment offers. There may be times when installment purchases are unavoidable, but this kind of spending, if excessive, can become a costly way of providing for family needs or for achieving family goals.

4. Take good care of your assets.

Clothes last longer and remain better looking if they are kept clean and pressed. Food lasts longer when it is properly stored. Equipment lasts longer and gives better service when used according to the manufacturer's instructions. It makes sense to prolong the use of one's possessions by taking care of them. The longer we can use an item, the more we are getting for our money.

5. Update your homeowner's policy.

As a rule, you need to be covered for at least 80 percent of the cost of rebuilding your house. Otherwise you won't get full reimbursement even if a fire destroys only one room. Ask your insurance agent how to estimate the cost. If you rent, get tenant's insurance to cover furniture and other valuables. Many renters fail to do this, thinking losses will be covered by the landlord. Not so!

6. Update your life insurance policy.

You need only enough to take care of your dependents if you die. If there is a non-bread winner in the family, generally stick with low-cost term insurance; then cut it back or cancel it when the children grow up. Primary breadwinners, by contrast, often have to provide for an aging spouse, so they may need some insurance whose premiums won't rise as they get older. If you have no dependents, you don't need life insurance. Put cash into retirement funds or disability insurance instead. Disability insurance is overlooked by many people.

7. Start a retirement fund.

If you work for a corporation which has one, use the 401(k) plan. If employed by a firm with no pension plan, open an Individual Retirement Account. As a rule, both the contributions to these plans and the earnings are untaxed until you withdraw the money, so tax savings help pay the cost. If you leave your job, you can take 401(k) savings with you. Do not fail to use these plans! They're the best route to independence in old age.

8. Get the best health insurance possible.

If you aren't covered at work, try to participate in a group plan through an organization you belong to or can join. Alternatively, call Blue Cross/Blue Shield or a Health Maintenance Organization (check the yellow pages). If you can't afford what they offer, talk to an insurance agent about a high deductible policy that covers only major medical costs. (You pay the small bills, but the huge ones are covered.)

Today's buyers often take deductibles of $1,000 to $5,000, which greatly lowers the cost of insurance premiums. Whatever you do, never buy insurance advertised by celebrities on TV; it's not worth the cost.

9. Pay off your home mortgage faster.

All over America, homeowners are taking 15 year mortgages or making extra payments on long-term mortgages, which has the effect of shortening the term. Any homeowner who has taken a look at an amortization schedule realizes that a large part of their monthly payment merely covers the interest charges on the outstanding debt, instead of paying down on the original loan.

Faster payments do lower interest costs and allow you to own your home free and clear sooner. A paid-up home is the cheapest way to live in retirement. By making slightly larger monthly payments than your loan requires, you'll significantly reduce your total interest cost and pay off your mortgage years early. For example, send in $50 extra in advance every month on a $150,000, 30-year, ten percent mortgage and you'll save $68,325 and reduce the term of your loan by more than five years. In recent years, interest rates on mortgages have dropped considerably. A mortgage balance with a six or seven percent interest obligation saves a lots of dollars as well.

While it is true that mortgage interest can offset your taxable income, this has limited value. The offset does not reduce the tax itself, rather it reduces taxable income. If you are in the twenty-eight percent tax bracket, a $100 mortgage-interest deduction will save $28 in federal taxes, $31 for you if you are in the thirty-one percent tax bracket and so on. The remaining part of that $100 mortgage ($72 or $69) interest payment is lost. Additionally, people with adjusted incomes well over $125,000 may not be allowed to deduct all of their mortgage interest.

Instead of making only the minimum payment required by a lender, many people today are repaying their loans more quickly. One way to do this is to use a fifteen-year rather than a thirty-year amortization schedule.

Another way is to prepay the mortgage either by making extra payments or by increasing the size of the regularly scheduled payments and specifying that the surplus should be applied to principal.

According to one source, adding a mere $10 a month to each payment, beginning in the third year of a $100,000 thirty-year mortgage at eight percent, can save $8,515 in interest charges and will pay off the debt sixteen months early.

If you will make just one prepayment of principal a year can make a tremendous difference over time. Starting with the same $100,000 loan at 8% for 30 years, a prepayment of $500 each December will cause the mortgage to be paid off 29 months early, while one-time annual prepayments of $1,000 and $2,000 will retire debt in 22 years, 7 months and 18 years, 8 months, respectively.

These results are so dramatic that it might seem as if every homeowner should begin prepaying immediately. But don't forget to first have six to twelve months of income set aside as an emergency fund.

10. Use non-money resources.

It is very easy to rely entirely on financial resources for all the goods one wants and needs. But this kind of thinking and living places a very heavy burden on the family income and often postpones the day when a goal can be achieved. However, by developing skills among family members and by substituting one's time, energy and skill in place of money, many services can be provided at home without dipping into the family funds. This kind of planning and achieving often provides far greater satisfaction than does the routine of shopping and buying.

11. If you want it to last, choose quality over price.

Do you look for quality rather than just cost or appearance when you buy something that you want to last a long time? Do you save sales receipts, guarantees and other records of purchases so you know where to find them? Do you buy at brand names stores that stand behind their merchandise?

Read the labels on boxes, packages or other purchases to determine the real quantity or quality you are getting for your money. Instead of purchasing your wants immediately, put money aside to save for something you want but can't afford at the moment.

12. Pause before purchasing.

Before spending your hard-earned resources, pause a while to ask yourself three simple questions.

- Can I really afford it?

- Do I really need it?

Whether or not you can afford it may be a simple matter of addition and subtraction; you either have enough money or you don't. But more often it will be a matter of deciding how important this particular purchase is compared to other purchases you may want to make.

There are many things we might like to have which would make life easier and more fun. Don't think you must always deny yourself all of these; after all, life is supposed to be fun as well as work.

Many things that would have been considered luxuries in past years are now considered necessities. But you are going to have to pick and choose according to whatever your particular desires are. The more limited your budget, the more picking and choosing you are going to have to do. This is one of the harder facts of life.

- Is it worth what I'm paying for it?

This is where spending money becomes a real skill. Worth or value is often hard to determine. Value in this case means the quality of the product itself; it also means the usefulness of the product for your particular purposes. You have to think about both.

In determining value, price alone can be misleading. The lowest price may be the best value for your money, but then again it may not be. The highest price doesn't necessarily mean the best value either. Usually, you will find the best value somewhere in between.

Generally, when you are buying a product where length of service and performance are important, quality (how well it is made, how well it functions, how long it will last) is first consideration. Price is (within budget limits) a second consideration. Appearance may or may not be a consideration. If it's a suit or dress, yes; if it's an electric drill, probably not.

If you are buying a product where length of service is not so important…soap or paper plates, for instance…the lower price is usually the better value for your purposes. Quality is not as important, as long as what you buy does the job to your satisfaction.

A lot of hard work and a little luck will stretch your dollars a little more.

13. You can save by putting yourself to work:

    ✦   Borrow books from your local public library instead of buying them.

    ✦   Buy a used car rather than a new one.

    ✦   Eat out at lunchtime rather than at dinner—it is usually at least 40 percent cheaper.

    ✦   Practice the art of trading down: one step down in suits, in travel arrangements, in size of rental cars, etc.

    ✦   Review insurance policies to avoid overlapping coverage.

    ✦   Take up walking or jogging in the park or the street and avoid the cost of joining a health club. Use free city parks and tennis courts, instead of paid recreational areas.

14. Understand inflation.

The rise in the price of goods and services, better known as inflation, can steadily erode the purchasing power of your income. That's why it's important to invest a portion of your savings. Inflation has been relatively tame in recent years. Since 1960, inflation has averaged 4.5

percent per year. Since 1988, it has averaged 3.5 percent per year. Still, no one can predict the direction of inflation rates, which could decline even more or return to the double-digit rates of the late 1970's and early 1980's. Even if inflation holds steady at 3.5 percent per year for 20 years, consumer prices will nearly double.

15. Understand the power of compounding.

Inflation can steadily erode the value of your income. Long-term investing offers the best antidote to inflation through the power of compounding.

Year after year, any money that you invest may earn interest, dividends or capital gains. When you reinvest those earnings, they help generate additional earnings. Those additional earnings help generate more earnings and so on. This is called compounding.

For example, if an investment returns 8 percent per year and its earnings are reinvested annually:

- After one year, your total return will be 8 percent.

- After five years, your cumulative total return will be 47 percent.

- After ten years, your cumulative total return will be 116 percent.

Best of all, the sooner you begin investing, the greater the compounding effect.

16. Begin saving while you are young.

Consider the example of Dick and Jane, both 65 years old. They worked for the same company for 35 years and both invested in their employer-sponsored retirement plan. Jane started contributing at age 30. She invested $1,000 each year for ten years until the age of 40 and earned 8 percent per year. Then she stopped contributing; her investment continued to earn an 8 percent annual return. When she reached age 65, her $10,000 had grown to $107,100.

Dick postponed making contributions until age 40 and then invested $1,000 each year for 25 years. He also earned 8 percent per year. At the end of the period, his $25,000 investment was worth $79,000.

As you can see, although Jane contributed to her company plan for 15 fewer years than Dick and invested $15,000 less, she accumulated $28,100 more than Dick—simply because she started investing ten years earlier.

17. Learn how to invest.

Saving and investing are often used interchangeably, but they are somewhat different. Saving is storing money safely—such as in a bank or money market account—for short-term needs such as upcoming expenses or emergencies. Typically, you earn a low, fixed rate of return and can withdraw your money easily.

Investing is taking a risk with a portion of your savings—such as by buying stocks or bonds—in hopes of realizing higher long-term returns. Unlike bank savings, stocks and bonds over the long term have returned enough to outpace inflation, but they also decline in value from time to time.

UNDERSTANDING INVESTMENT RISK

First of all, it is necessary to understand investment risk. No get-rich scheme will ever bring you peace and security. No method of investing, no category of investing, and no investment vehicle will shorten the time needed to see a financial return.

If someone insists that they have a way for you to easily make a greater than average return on any investment, hang up the phone or turn and run in the other direction. With regard to your money, there will always be someone more than willing to separate you from it. Just remember that hot tips lead to burnt fingers.

If you're like many investors, you want to get the highest possible return on your investments while assuming the least amount of risk. Unfortunately, finding a comfortable balance between risk and reward can be difficult.

When planning your investment strategy, you need to determine your risk tolerance level. The amount of risk you can handle in your portfolio depends on several factors; your age, family situation, your current income and your financial goals. The amount of risk you are willing to assume can help you determine the types of investments you may include in your portfolio.

There are several types of risk that every portfolio can be exposed to. Investment gains and losses can result from such factors as economic conditions and changes in the financial markets. In building your portfolio, you should be aware of some of the categories of risk.

LIQUIDITY RISK

Liquidity risk means not being able to liquidate an investment quickly while keeping the original investment amount intact. This can occur with investing in bonds where the bond must be held to maturity in order for you to achieve a specific interest return.

It can also be a risk should you invest in a particular stock, but find that the price is down at the same time you need to get your hands on the cash invested in that specific equity. For this reason, any dollars you need to access for the purpose of educational spending or maybe the purchase of a house should never be invested in the equities market.

INFLATION RISK

Inflation risk is the danger that inflation will reduce the purchasing power of your investment over time. Low-yielding investments such as savings accounts and money market funds may not earn enough to outpace rising prices.

ECONOMIC RISK

Economic risk can surface due to the fact that slow economic growth will be too weak to sustain or improve the return on a particular investment. For example, the price of shares in growth companies that require a strong economy to sustain earnings may fall during an economic slowdown.

Again, as in the case of liquidity risk, you would not want to invest any dollars required for education or other short-term needs into an investment that would have a substantial economic risk attached to it.

INTEREST RATE RISK

Interest rate risk occurs when changes in interest rates cause the value of certain investments to decrease. For example, when interest rates rise, the market value of fixed-income securities, such as bonds, declines.

Bond investors hate inflation because it erodes the value of bonds' fixed interest payments. Investors are locked into the lower rate as the market rates rise. However, this type of risk may hold less potential for major financial damage.

MARKET RISK

Market risk is the risk associated with market fluctuations that can depress the value of particular investments. All stocks and bonds can be affected by downturns caused by fraud, war, or calamity. Additionally, certain types of investments can experience a major downturn should there be a slowdown in a specific industry or category of investments.

Factors such as political developments, market cycles, changing investor sentiments or reaction to previous excessive rises or declines can all contribute to market volatility. Higher interest rates hurt stocks because they can slow the economy, which can crimp a company's revenue. They boost corporate borrowing costs and make stocks less attractive relative to interest-paying investments.

COMPANY RISK

If a company's stock value decreases due to financial difficulties, this creates an instant company risk. Internal factors such as inefficient production and poor management or external factors such as problems with the industry, the economy, or trade can contribute to company risk.

SPECIFIC RISK

Specific risk involves any occurrences that may affect only a particular company. For example, the death of the founder, political developments, or heavy debt can affect a particular firm adversely. Some huge companies that have been around for a very long time, even with great products and unsoiled reputations, have fallen into the wrong hands and ended up worthless due to fraud and misrepresentation.

PRINCIPLE THREE

DIMINISHING YOUR INVESTMENT RISK

R isk is not something you should try to eliminate from your portfolio. However, you must manage your risk. By choosing only ultra conservative investments, you limit the potential return on your investments. Instead, minimize your risk by diversifying your portfolio and choosing investments that will bring you peace of mind as well as your desired rate of return.

You can manage your investment risk through proper diversification, also known as asset allocation. In our world of uncertainty, it makes sense to reduce your risks wherever possible. This is especially true when it comes to investing.

That's what diversification does. It's a way to reduce exposure to risk without reducing your potential for return. Diversification is the spreading of your money into a variety of investments. Changes in economic conditions affect some securities differently, but the impact of any single asset category is minimized.

Through diversification, you distribute your assets among a variety of investment categories and, thus, spread your risk. Of course, your personal situation and investment goals will affect the way in which you diversify your portfolio. You need to discern your objectives based on your age, family obligations, income needs, liquidity requirements, tax considerations, and tolerance for risk.

When you're determining your asset mix, consider these four types of diversification: across asset classes, across time horizons, across industries, and among companies.

DIVERSIFICATION ACROSS TYPES OF SECURITIES

Investing among different categories of securities such as stocks, bonds, mutual funds, U.S. Treasuries, or money market instruments allows you to reduce your portfolio's exposure to any single part of the market. This type of diversification is also known as asset allocation.

The key to asset allocation is understanding how different categories of assets react to various market changes in relation to one another. One such correlation is that, during an economic downturn, most stocks tend to perform poorly. However, a slow economy can have just the opposite effect on the bond market.

Because a sluggish economic environment is usually accompanied by lower interest rates, bonds will typically rise in value during an economic downturn. Therefore, by holding some stocks and some bonds, you can lessen the effects of economic volatility on your overall portfolio.

DIVERSIFICATION ACROSS TIME HORIZONS

While investing among different asset classes is important, proper diversification requires tailoring your portfolio to your needs. Investing across varying investment time horizons is the way to build a portfolio that is suited to your objectives, without sacrificing diversification.

For example, certificates of deposit, money market funds, and Treasury bills have relatively short time horizons. Other investments, like growth stocks, have long time horizons.

Investments with short time horizons can give your portfolio an anchor of stability. However, if your portfolio is too heavily weighted in these asset classes, you take the risk of reduced return because of declining interest rates or increased inflation.

On the other hand, investments with longer time horizons can result in significant capital appreciation in your portfolio. Stocks, for example, have historically been the best performing asset class over the long term. However, stocks require a long-term orientation in order to smooth out market volatility, the ups and downs of the market.

Historically, the stock market has had up to four consecutive years of a declining market. This can devastate any portfolio immediately. If your need for money occurs during that time, not only will you lose on your investment, you may even incur substantial losses. Being too heavily weighted in investments with a long time horizon can deprive your portfolio of stability, as well as safety for emergency cash reserves over the short term. The best approach is to hold some long-term and some short-term investments to reduce overall fluctuation in your portfolio.

DIVERSIFICATION ACROSS INDUSTRIES

You can further diversify your portfolio by investing in companies in a variety of different industries. This reduces industry risk, the risk that an entire grouping of business will under-perform the market.

By dividing your portfolio among several industries, you ensure that its performance won't depend entirely on one type of business. Volatility in one industry will have only a negligible effect on your portfolio because you've spread your risk.

DIVERSIFICATION AMONG DIFFERENT COMPANIES

Within industries, it can make sense to diversify among stocks of different companies. This reduces what professionals call credit risk. This is the risk that any one company will experience difficulties because of factors such as poor management, a lack of market for their products or services, or the superiority of competition. It also reduces your risk should fraud and mismanagement be perpetrated by company management.

INVESTING MISTAKES TO AVOID

There are a number of mistakes that many of us make when it comes to managing our finances. While it is always very easy to make mistakes, it can be very hard to live with the consequences. One thing we should try to avoid is making the same mistake twice. Here are some very real pitfalls to be aware of.

FAILING TO SET GOALS

Without clear targets, you will lack motivation to save and invest. But remember: all your objectives need not be high-minded or long term. Small victories pave the road to larger successes. In fact, many financial advisors find that a good way to get in the habit of moving toward goals is to establish a few near-term achievable ones with pleasurable payoffs, such as saving for a trip to Hawaii, the Caribbean, Barbados or Idaho!

Small rewards and extravagances can be very nice. There can be great incentive in setting aside some cash for these personal getaways. Once you've set your aims, establish an unshakable routine for putting aside cash to keep on track.

GIVING UP ALL DECISIONS TO AN ADVISOR

Yes, it's okay to hire a tax professional to handle your state and federal returns or a stockbroker to suggest investments, but no one knows as much about or is as interested in your finances as you are. Take advantage of that fact and devote the couple of hours a week or so that financial planners say is required for most people to stay on top of their money.

FAILING TO FIND A SENSIBLE INVESTMENT STRATEGY

Most people build an investment portfolio the same way they collect shells at the beach. They pick up whatever happens to strike their eye. It may be a hot tip from a friend or a friend of a friend, a slick magazine advertisement or a fancy, colored brochure. As a result, they wind up with investments that often reflect only the fashion of the moment, not their goals or their investing temperament.

Decide first how much risk you are willing to take and then look for investments that will let you sleep at night and provide the return you need to meet your target on time. Unless you are starting very late in working toward your major objectives, you should be able to find investments well within your comfort zone.

Remember that your investment style should reflect the time you have to devote to it and your financial expertise. If you don't know much about picking stocks or bonds or if you cannot spend a couple of hours a week researching individual equity issues, put your money in mutual funds or hire a money manager.

FAILING TO UNDERSTAND RISK AND DIVERSIFY ADEQUATELY

Investors often focus on one or two obvious risks and neglect to protect themselves against other threats. For example, if you invest the bulk of your assets in Treasury bills to avoid risks in the stock and bond markets, your returns may not keep you adequately ahead of inflation long term.

The solution is have a well-balanced portfolio of investments with different traits, such as stocks, bonds, money-market funds, real estate and, perhaps, precious metals.

TRYING TO TIME THE STOCK MARKET

Few investors, professionals included, can catch a climbing stock or mutual fund just before it takes off, or can bail out at precisely the right instant. So don't try. Instead, be a buy-and-hold investor.

DRIVING YOUR INVESTMENT STRATEGY WITH TAXES

Don't allow attractive tax advantages to blind you to an investment's basic strengths and weaknesses. Before you buy a product that promises to save you taxes, compare it with taxable alternatives. To find out how much a taxable investment would have to return to edge out a tax-exempt one, use this formula.

Divide the tax-exempt yield you are considering by 1 minus your tax bracket expressed as a decimal. So if you are in the 28 percent federal tax bracket and want to find out how much you'd have to earn from a taxable asset to equal the return on a tax-exempt investment yielding 7 percent, divide 7 by 0.72 (1 - 0.28).

Conclusion: to beat the return on the tax-exempt investment, you'd need to earn more than 9.72 percent on a taxable one.

Aggressively Seeking the Highest Yield

Trying to catch the highest yield is a strategy that can work well in the risk-free confines of savings accounts and CDs. However, in any other area you can very quickly chase high yields down a very deep hole. That's because in more variable income investments such as bonds and bond mutual funds, the interest payments (which determine your yield) make up only part of your total return.

The other part is the change in the value of your principal. A drop in a bond or a bond fund's principal value (because of rising interest rates or a default) can reduce and even wipe out any higher yield it may have offered. If you only search for high yields, you may not always get high total returns; and total return is the only true measure of whether you've made money.

Relying on Past Performance Only for Investment Choices

The problem with pursuing hot performers is that last year's star all too frequently turns out to be this year's dog. The lesson to be learned here is to judge investments on future prospects, not past successes.

Underestimating the Effect of Commissions

High fees and commissions can reduce the value of your investments and financial services very fast. Costs that sometimes sound insignificant can add up.

If you are over the age of 50 and put $5,000 into an Individual Retirement Account in a mutual fund that has a no-load, low-expense policy, you'll be miles ahead of placing the same dollars in a fund with an 8.5 percent load and a 2 percent annual expense cost.

FAILING TO KEEP ACCURATE TAX RECORDS

Yes, it's a pain when you first begin this task! Accurate records can help you cut taxes by reminding you of deductible expenditures. They can also help you weed out poor investments. And, of course, they will aid your heirs after you're gone.

NOT SETTING ASIDE ADEQUATE CASH FOR EMERGENCIES

Make sure you've stashed six to twelve months' worth of living expenses in an account that allows fast withdrawals without penalty. The best place for the extra money is in a money-market mutual fund.

UNDERESTIMATING YOUR RETIREMENT OBLIGATIONS

In planning for retirement, few people pay enough attention to two potential time bombs: their own life expectancy and inflation. At age 60, according to those who know, the median life expectancy is 20 years for a man and 25 for a women. But those are only medians and, for that reason, you really need to plan for 30 years or so.

And in far less time than that, inflation can make sizable savings seem insignificant. According to experts, if living costs rise at a moderate 5 percent, a pension payment of $1,000 a month when you were 60 would have only $277 of today's purchasing power when you hit 85.

Excessive Worrying about the Small Things

Be cost-conscious, but don't fret. If your neighbor's bank CD pays a quarter of a point more in interest than yours, don't worry about it. That deal will earn him or her just $2.50 more this year pretax for each $1,000 invested. Instead, focus on your goals and on carrying out a long-term strategy for reaching them.

PRINCIPLE FIVE

STEPS TO SUCCESSFUL INVESTING

T he following are a few guidelines and suggestions on investing that may be helpful. They represent sound ways to grow a portfolio while providing adequate built-in safeguards for long-term preservation.

ESTABLISH INVESTMENT OBJECTIVES AND STICK WITH THEM

Periodically, stock funds take a hammering. But over long spans of time, stocks as a group have consistently come up winners. Measured over 20-year periods, stretching all the way back to 1871, stocks beat bonds 94 percent of the time and cash 99 percent of the time.

Cash isn't the stuff you carry around in your wallet; rather, it refers to safe, readily-accessible assets like Treasury bills and money-market funds. Since 1926, there have been many bull and bear markets. Yet, throughout the entire period, common stocks have returned an after-inflation (the only return that really counts) average of 7 percent annually, according to Jeremy J. Siegel, a Wharton School finance professor. This compares to long-term government bond's paltry 1.7 percent and Treasury bills with an after-inflation return of 0.5 percent.

For patient investors, stocks have built up an overwhelming advantage over other investments. What does that mean for the average investor? When the newspapers and networks proclaim doom and gloom with headlines about uncertainty, one needs to place them into perspective and remain committed to long-term objectives.

INVEST FOR THE LONG TERM

You have heard that patience is a virtue? It is especially true when it comes to investing anything of value, whether it be your time, your support, or your money. Patience is a key ingredient to investment success. Long-term investing can pay off very nicely despite fluctuations in value over the short term.

According to many financial professionals, stock investments have a long-term growth rate well in excess of bonds, Treasury securities and inflation. For any 20-year period during the last six decades, the S & P 500 has never experienced a loss on an inflation-adjusted basis.

In fact, short-term downturns often present excellent long-term investment opportunities. Historically, investors have often realized their biggest gains during market panics. So it makes sense to increase your equity positions when everyone else is selling out. If you have short-term objectives, keep investment maturities short.

STAY INVESTED

An investor needs to leave his/her money invested for compounding to work to its fullest. The importance of time to investment success is illustrated by the Rule of 72. This commonly used mathematical formula bears repeating here.

To estimate the amount of time it takes money to double, you divide 72 by the assumed interest rate. Assuming a 7.5 percent annual rate of return, an investment of $5,000 today will grow to $10,000 in nine and one-half years. By staying invested for the long term, you can be assured that you will not miss out on the next bull market.

PRACTICE DOLLAR-COST AVERAGING

How courageous of an investor are you? Do you see yourself as a risk-taker? Have you ever tried to beat the market and lost? Do you have the courage to buy stocks only after prices have risen sharply, then find yourself selling them after prices have already fallen?

There is a simple way to avoid these investment pitfalls: a periodic investing technique called dollar-cost averaging. By investing a fixed amount on a regular basis, an investor can avoid the difficulty of deciding the best times to invest.

Another result of investing the same dollar amount each period is that you automatically purchase fewer shares of an investment when prices are high and more shares when prices are low.

In this way, you can help lower your average cost per share over the course of your investment plan. Of course, like any investment strategy, dollar-cost averaging is not foolproof. It neither assures a profit nor protects against losses in a declining market.

In addition, such a plan involves continuous investments in stocks and mutual funds regardless of fluctuating price levels. An investor should always consider his or her financial ability to continue their purchasing through periods of low price levels.

A PROVERB AND AN EXAMPLE

We can understand the principle of dollar-cost averaging by taking a look at the following biblical proverb:

"Steady plodding brings prosperity; hasty speculation brings poverty" (Proverbs 21:5 *TLB*).

Dollar-cost averaging takes the guesswork out of timing the ups and downs of the stock and bond markets. This time-tested method for systematic investing can be a particularly good approach in today's uncertain investment environment. Dollar-cost averaging eliminates emotional investment decisions and provides a regular and disciplined investment program.

Dollar-cost averaging involves investing a fixed amount of money at regular intervals, such as monthly, quarterly or annually. By investing on a dollar basis at regular intervals, rather than buying a fixed number of shares, an investor can purchase more shares when prices are low and fewer when prices are high.

Short-term price decreases are viewed as buying opportunities, assuming that the investment will eventually rebound. The result... the average cost per share is typically lower.

Dollar-cost averaging also enables a person to get into the habit of investing regularly. This is one way to strive toward long-term saving targets, such as college tuition or retirement.

The key to investing in anything, especially the stock market, is to set aside regular amounts for systematic investment. Market timing is not science but rather wishful thinking. In fact, some have suggested that most individual investors do not buy low and sell high. They seem to buy high and sell low. After all, it takes real courage to buy when the stock market is low, the news is bad, and the future looks bleak. That's the time when most individuals sell out.

The following illustration of dollar-cost averaging will show us its principle and its power. To simply our explanation, let's place an initial per share price point of $10 per share. Let us say for example that the price of one share of a mutual fund selling at $10 a share drops by as much as 50 percent over a period of one year. Now obviously this would be a bad situation to have happen after you purchase your initial shares;

actually a very devastating one and the kind that might influence you to sell out at the bottom.

But then, let's imagine that you continued to have confidence in the holdings of this mutual fund and in its management team, so you continue to invest $100 in the mutual fund every time the share price dropped another $1.00 per share.

As the mutual fund share price drops all the way to $5, you continue to invest monthly at each price point and then continue to do so as it recovers to the initial starting point of $10.

This is certainly not an example of a bull market and yet, what will have happened overall will be very satisfactory. Notice the results of $100 invested each month for eleven months, at each point down the ladder and back up again to the original price.

➤ Month #1: Investing an additional $100 at a cost of $10 each buys 10 shares.

➤ Month #2: Investing an additional $100 at a cost of $9 each buys 11.111 shares.

➤ Month #3: Investing an additional $100 at a cost of $8 each buys 12.5 shares.

➤ Month #4: Investing an additional $100 at a cost of $7 each buys 14.286 shares.

➤ Month #5: Investing an additional $100 at a cost of $6 each buys 16.667 shares.

➤ Month #6: Investing an additional $100 at a cost of $5 each buys 20 shares.

➤ Month #7: Investing an additional $100 at a cost of $6 each buys 16.667 shares.

➤ Month #8: Investing an additional $100 at a cost of $7 each buys 14.286 shares.

➤ Month #9: Investing an additional $100 at a cost of $8 each buys 12.5 shares.

➤ Month #10: Investing an additional $100 at a cost of $9 each buys 11.111 shares.

➤ Month #11: Investing an additional $100 at a cost of $10 each buys 10 shares.

The final total of dollars you would have invested = $1,100

The total number of shares you would now have = 149.128.

The total value of your shares at the end of the year (149.128 X $10) = $1,491.28.

The total gain on your investment at the point that the share price recovers would be 35.6 percent.

At no point did the stock ever sell above your initial buying price, but in the end you had a 35 percent profit. And this does not include whatever dividend the mutual fund may have paid. This is the value of dollar-cost averaging!

The above illustration is, of course, hypothetical. An investor should realize that no investment program can assure a profit or protect against loss in declining markets.

Discontinuing the program during a period when the market value of shares is less than original cost would incur a loss.

For this reason, any investor contemplating such a program should take into account his or her ability to continue it during any such period. Keep in mind that sometimes a stock loses value and never regains its original price.

This is the reason the example used was a stock mutual fund. It would be less likely to stay at the lower price levels. Although dollar-cost averaging is a good investment tool, investors must realize that no method guarantees a risk-free investment. The value of holdings will only be determined by what a buyer is willing to invest.

PRINCIPLE SIX

MUTUAL FUND INVESTING

I t is a fact that a safer way to invest in a wide range of equities is to invest in them through a mutual fund holding. Achieving proper diversification is often difficult for investors purchasing individual securities. For example, many professionals recommend investing in a minimum of 15 stocks in order to have a properly diversified equity portfolio.

This can require a capital investment which simply isn't feasible for many people. Moreover, researching and monitoring a large stock portfolio can be a cumbersome chore. That is why so many investors turn to mutual funds, which are an affordable and convenient way to diversify your portfolio. Mutual funds are designed to meet specifically stated investment goals. With such diversification, an individual may own many more issues in their particular asset class.

Many funds target a specific industry sector, investing in many stocks across that sector. For instance, there are mutual funds which invest in stocks of small, emerging companies and other funds which emphasize investments in securities of international companies.

Shareholders who invest a few hundred dollars in a mutual fund receive the same investment return, the same professional management, and the same diversification as those who invest much more.

Professional managers of the fund are able to invest the fund's assets in a variety of securities, targeting hot industries and selecting the best individual stocks within those industries. This approach to investing allows the individual to reduce risk while participating in the opportunities offered.

4 PRINCIPLES FOR WISE INVESTING

The Principle of Seeking Out Low Cost Funds

In the 90's, gains-hungry investors paid no more attention to fund expenses than drag racers do to gas mileage. Who cared about costs as long as stock funds were piling up average annual gains of over 15 percent and bond funds were churning out 10 percent or more a year?

In the present decade, when analysts expect yearly returns to be three to five points lower, fees and expenses will be larger, increasing losses and slowing subsequent recoveries. For instance, according to Money Magazine, a no-load fund with a 9.75 percent gross return and a low 0.75 percent annual expense ratio would build $10,000 into $23,670 over the next 10 years. A 4 percent load fund with a stiff 1.5 percent charge would knock that down to $21,210.

As a rule, avoid domestic stock funds with annual expenses that total more than 1.5 percent of assets. In evaluating international funds, in which the cost of doing business overseas increases fees, cut out any fund charging more than 2 percent a year. With bond funds, insist on expenses below 1 percent.

The Principle of Dollar-Cost Averaging

Investing a fixed amount of money at regular intervals—say, $100 to $500 a month—takes much of the risk out of stock funds, with little effort. For one thing, it prevents you from committing your total dollars available at a market peak. And if your fund's share value does drop, your next installment payment automatically picks up more of the lower-priced shares. That cuts your average cost per share and boosts your eventual gain.

The Principle of Building a Well-Balanced and Diversified Portfolio

Most investors are familiar with the don't-put-all-your-eggs-in-one-basket logic of diversification. Fewer really understand how powerful a risk-reducing tactic it is. Sensible diversification costs you relatively little in performance.

Analysts say that you should divide your money among funds with different styles. Over any investment period of 10 years or more, funds with differing investment philosophies will take turns outperforming—and being outperformed by those with other philosophies. Some experts suggest that you put 20-40 percent of your stockholdings into value funds. Value investing typically pays off best at the end of a bear market and in the early part of a new bull market.

By diversifying among funds, you acknowledge the unpredictability of markets and lessen the damage if you're wrong. In an uncertain market, diversification is king. Whatever happens, if your money is spread among assets and investment styles, you should be able to sleep at night.

The Principle of Understanding Market Indexes

Index funds allow individual investors to do what many corporate pension fund managers have accomplished successfully for years: invest passively in diversified stock portfolios that closely match the performance of major market yardsticks. In general, the funds that track indexes of larger capitalization stocks (such as the S&P 500) provide moderate growth with relatively low risk. In contrast, indexes of smaller capitalization stocks (for example, the Russell 2000) should demonstrate faster growth but greater volatility.

The index fund approach has two distinct advantages. First, it provides a high degree of performance predictability relative to the market as a whole and second, it does this at low cost. Expenses are low because management advisory fees generally are modest. And since fund holdings are turned over infrequently, capital gains distributions, commissions costs and operating expenses are low, enhancing net returns to shareholders.

Index funds have their drawbacks. In a slumping market, a passive strategy may fare worse than that of a conventional fund whose manager builds up a large cash reserve. However, index funds represent a relatively conservative investment option for those who are willing to ride out unpredictable market swings in expectation of long-term appreciation.

Various indexes that measure the performance of the U.S. Market range from the broadest perspective to a narrow look at a single industry. Still other indexes track foreign stock markets. Several major domestic indexes are profiled below with information from Standard and Poor's.

S & P COMPOSITE INDEX: When investment professionals want a stand-in for the general market, they usually turn to the S&P 500. As the name indicates, the index consists of 500 U.S. issues, which represent about 70 percent of the total market value of American stocks. The 500 is capitalization-weighted, meaning that stocks influence the index in proportion to their importance in the market. The S&P 100 is simply the top 20 percent of the 500.

DOW JONES INDUSTRIAL AVERAGE: The oldest measure of market performance, the DJIA took its modern form of 30 large-capitalization stocks in 1928. The original version of Charles Dow's average, which consisted of only 11 stocks (nine of them railroads), first appeared in 1884. Originally the average price of a set of stocks, calculation of the DJIA has been changed over the years to reflect stock splits and substitutions.

Two other market averages from Dow Jones track specific sectors. The Transportation average is composed of 20 airline, railroad and trucking companies, while the Utility average consists of 15 gas and electric companies. All three averages are included in the Dow Jones 65 Stocks Composite.

NYSE COMPOSITE INDEX: This index measures the combined change in the value of all common stocks listed on the New York Stock Exchange. The base value was set at 50 as of year-end 1965. (That value was chosen because it was close to the average price of a NYSE-listed share at the time.) Four sub-indexes of NYSE-listed stocks are also tracked: Industrial, Transportation, Utility and Finance.

AMEX MARKET VALUE INDEX: Established in September 1973, the AMEX Market Value Index measures the change in value of roughly 1,000 issues traded on the American Stock Exchange. Included are common shares, ADRs and warrants. The Amex index has eight industry subgroups and another eight geographic subgroups, the latter reflecting corporate headquarters locations. The Market Value Index treats cash dividends as reinvested, thereby providing a picture of the total return for Amex stocks.

NASDAQ COMPOSITE INDEX: This is a measure of all OTC (Over The Counter) issues (except warrants) traded on the NASDAQ National Market System (NMS) and all domestic non-NMS common stocks traded in the regular NASDAQ market. The composite and its six sub-indexes (Industrial, Banks, Insurance, Other Finance, Transportation and Utilities) are market-value weighted. (Large companies move them more than smaller companies.) Cash dividends are not counted in the indexes. The NASDAQ Composite and its sub-indexes were established in 1971.

RUSSELL 1000, 2000, 3000: These indexes were developed by the Frank Russell Company to track the 3000 most actively traded U.S. shares. The Russell 3000 contains all of the issues, is capitalization-weighted and represents about 99 percent of the stocks held in institutional portfolios. The 1000 is the top tier of the domestic market and the 2000 represents the second tier.

WILSHIRE 5000: Although called the Wilshire 5000, this index actually tracks the value of more than 6,000 domestic stock issues. Established in 1974 by Wilshire Associates, this capitalization weighted index is designed to represent the total value of the U.S. market.

S & P MIDCAP 400: The newest addition to the index universe is the S&P MidCap 400, which was launched in recent years. Designed to track that segment of the market just below the 500, the S&P MidCap 400 is a market-weighted index. Unlike the 500, the S&P MidCap 400 has no industry sub-indexes.

PRINCIPLE SEVEN

INVESTMENT ALTERNATIVES

While we have discussed many investment possibilities up to this point, now a succinct summary of all of the various alternatives is provided next.

INVESTMENT IN CASH

Cash investments are short-term debt instruments that you can convert into cash easily, with little or no cost or penalty. They are sometimes called short-term reserves, cash reserves or cash. Examples include money market mutual funds, bank checking accounts, certificates of deposit (CD's) and Treasury bills (T-bills). The advantages of cash investments are their stability of principal and liquidity. Disadvantages include inflation risk and income risk.

INVESTMENT IN BONDS

Bonds are debt securities issued by corporations or governments in exchange for money you lend them. In most instances, bond issuers agree to repay their loans by a specific date and to make regular interest payments to you until that date. That's why bonds are often referred to as fixed-income investments.

Bonds vary according to different criteria. One is the issuer. Bonds are issued by the U.S. Treasury, U.S. government agencies, corporations, and state or local governments. Another criteria is the bond maturity.

The maturity date is the date when the bond issuer agrees to repay you the principal or face value of the loan. Bonds can be short-term (less than 5 years), intermediate-term (5–10 years) or long-term (more than 10 years).

Another criteria of bonds is their credit quality. A bond's quality is measured by the issuer's ability to pay interest and repay principal in a timely manner. Treasury bonds have the highest credit quality because they are backed by the full faith and credit of the U.S. government. Corporate high-yield "junk" bonds have the lowest credit quality.

Advantages of investing in bonds include both current income and broad diversification possibilities. Disadvantages include interest rate risk, credit risk and call risk.

Interest rate risk means that the market value of your bonds could decline due to rising interest rates. (In general, bond prices fall when interest rates rise—and rise when interest rates fall.)

Credit risk can also affect the value of your bond investment. You could lose money if a bond issuer defaults, fails to make timely payments of principal and interest, or if a bond's credit rating is reduced.

Another possible disadvantage of investing in bonds is what is termed call risk. During periods of falling interest rates, corporate and municipal bond issuers may prepay or call their loans before maturity in order to reissue the loans at a lower rate. You as lender, then, must reinvest this prepaid principal sooner than you had anticipated—and possibly at a lower interest rate.

The last two possible disadvantages to investing in bonds are inflation risk and event risk. The danger of inflation risk is that the interest income you earn from a bond investment remains the same over the life of the bond. The value of that income could be eroded by inflation. With event risk, the credit quality or market value of your bonds could suffer in response to an event such as a merger, leveraged buyout or other corporate restructuring.

The list below explains some ratings for various levels of bonds and a description of their risks. As noted these come from both Standard &

Poor's and Moody's. When purchasing any kind of bond, always check the risk and rating. The actual return should be your last consideration.

Standard & Poor's	Moody's	Description
AAA	Aaa	Best quality, smallest degree of risk
AA	Aa	High quality, slightly more risk
A	A	Upper medium grade, possible risk
BBB	Baa	Medium grade, but not well-secured
BB	Ba	Speculative issues, moderate protection
B	B	Very Speculative, little protection
CCC	Caa	Issues in poor standing, may default
CC	Ca	Highly speculative, marked shortcomings
D	C	Lowest quality, in default

INVESTMENT IN TREASURY SECURITIES

Treasury securities are negotiable debt obligations issued by the U.S. government for a specific amount and maturity. The government issues three types of Treasuries:

➡ Treasury bills (T-bills), with a maturity of 1 year or less.

➡ Treasury notes (T-notes), with a maturity of 1 to 10 years.

➡ Treasury bonds (T-bonds), with a maturity of 10 to 30 years.

There is safety in the purchase of U.S. Treasury Securities. They are backed by the full faith and credit of the U.S. Government and are considered ideal for safeguarding and preserving capital.

If held to maturity, Treasuries are guaranteed to repay your original investment. No matter how volatile the market may be, you never risk your principal if you hold the security until the date of maturity.

Since Treasuries are a fixed-rate security, you'll know exactly what your income will be and when you will receive interest payments. When purchasing Treasury Notes or Bonds, you will receive a steady stream of income from the semiannual interest payments. Although Treasuries are federally taxable, the interest is exempt from both state and local taxes. Therefore, your after-tax return may be higher than the same yields on fully taxable investments, especially if you live in a high-tax state.

There is an active secondary market for Treasuries which trades billions of dollars every day. This enables you to trade your Treasury securities before maturity should you need to raise some quick cash. Of course, should you sell before maturity, you may realize either a gain or a loss on your investment, depending on market value when you sell. If interest rates have fallen, the value of the securities goes up and you'll most likely get back more than you anticipated. However, if the reverse is true, your return will probably fall short.

When buying Treasuries you have a lot of flexibility as to when you want the principal back. Whether you are saving for the children's education or your own retirement, you can target the exact date that you want the security to mature to meet your individual investment goals.

T-Bills are short-term instruments and have maturities of three and six months and one year. T-Notes mature in two, three, five, seven and ten years. T-Bonds have maturities of 11 to 30 years. STRIPS have maturities of six months to 30 years.

So what are Treasury Bills? Short-term Treasury Bills are sold at a discount and return their full face value at maturity. The interest you earn is the difference between the face value and the price you actually pay. The discount rate simply indicates the trading price and does not refer to the actual yield, which is always higher.

For example, if a one-year T-Bill is quoted at 7.72, the security is selling at a discount of 7.72 percent of $10,000, or $9,228. At maturity, you'd receive your original investment plus $772 in interest earned, for a yield of 8.37 percent. Treasury Bills can be an excellent investment alternative to savings accounts or CDs. Exempt from both state and local taxes, T-Bills not only protect your capital, but may also provide a better return than fully taxable alternatives.

Treasury Notes and Bonds

These securities pay interest semiannually and can provide the investor with a steady source of income. If held to maturity, intermediate T-Notes and T-Bonds both lock in a fixed rate of return that is guaranteed regardless of changes in market conditions.

Zero Coupon Bonds

Zero-Coupon Treasuries, or STRIPS, is another outstanding investment vehicle. The prospect of having to have a specific sum of money at a set point in time can be a worrisome dilemma. Whether it's your children's college tuition, your retirement, a wedding, dream vacation or a second home you are looking forward to, U.S. Treasury Zero Coupon Bonds can help to offer you an assured way to take what you have today and turn it into what you need for tomorrow.

They are sold at deep discounts and cost substantially less than their face value. Your return is the difference between what you pay for your STRIPS and what you receive at maturity. Zero Coupon Bonds make no regular interest payments. The interest on the STRIPS accrues over the life of the bond and is automatically reinvested so that you earn interest on both the interest and the principal. This compounding locks in a rate of return and enables a small initial investment to achieve dramatic growth if held to maturity.

You buy Zero Coupon Bonds at a small fraction of their $1,000 face amount — then redeem them at full value at maturity. For example, if you buy approximately $8,500 worth of 10 year Zero Coupon Bonds that pay 8.75 percent compounded semiannually, your $8,500 will grow to $20,000 at maturity.

This investment vehicle is thought to be just about the best way of knowing exactly how much a certain sum of money will grow to in a given number of years. And because there are so many maturity dates to pick from, you can select the maturity that matches the time you'll need the money and know precisely how much you'll have on that date.

Since STRIPS do offer a wide choice of maturities they are popular for investors who need a large lump sum at a specific future time, such as for college or retirement. Although interest isn't paid until the STRIPS mature, it is taxable the year it's credited to you. It is because of this that STRIPS are favored for tax-deferred accounts such as IRA's.

The predictability of zeros depends on your holding them until maturity. That's why they may be ideal for your IRA. All interest (if in an IRA account) accumulates tax-deferred until withdrawn at retirement, when your tax bracket is usually much lower.

Many individuals use zeros as a long-term savings tool. With some planning, you can purchase zeros that will mature during your retirement years. At that time, the return on your zeros will supplement other sources of retirement income (pensions, profit sharing plans and Social Security benefits).

Here is a quick look at different types of zeros. You can choose from a variety of zero coupon bonds. Many IRA investors opt for Treasury zeros or STRIPS. They offer the highest degree of safety because they are backed by the full faith and credit of the United States government and your return is guaranteed if held to maturity. They are also exempt from state and local taxes.

Corporate zeros tend to offer higher yields than Treasury zeros, but safety may be compromised. They are backed only by the issuing corporation. Corporates are rated by independent agencies, such as Moody's or Standard & Poor's, to indicate their level of credit risk at the time of purchase. In addition, corporate zeros may be called or bought back by the issuing company prior to the bond's stated maturity date, putting your principal at risk.

There are some tax issues to consider. In non-retirement accounts, zero-coupon bonds are subject to tax on so-called phantom income.

This means the annual buildup of interest from most zeros is taxed even though you do not actually receive any payment until maturity.

The amount taxed each year starts low and increases as the bond moves closer to maturity. In the case of an Individual Retirement Account, however, you avoid having the phantom interest included with your taxable income. You bypass paying yearly taxes on the accumulating interest and you only pay taxes when you withdraw your retirement funds.

As with all other types of investment opportunities and possibilities, there are both advantages and disadvantages to investing in treasury securities, but the overall benefits are substantial. First is the stability of principal. Next is the liquidity factor. Treasuries are considered to have the highest credit quality of all debt instruments and are therefore easily sold and converted to cash.

Not to be lost in the discussion of benefits is the call protection factor. Treasuries generally are not callable, which means the issuer cannot redeem the security before its scheduled maturity date. This feature locks in your interest rate until maturity. And one final benefit is the tax advantage. Income from treasury securities is exempt from state and local taxes (but not from federal income tax).

Every investment alternative has its particular downside. With treasuries, it is the interest rate risk. You are guaranteed only to receive timely payment of interest and repayment of principal upon maturity. Before maturity, however, the market value of your securities could decline due to rising interest rates.

There is also the possibility of less current income. Because they have high credit quality, treasuries provide less interest income than bonds with comparable maturities and lower credit quality. One final reminder is that bonds of all types are subject to inflation risk. The interest income you earn from a bond investment remains the same over the life of the bond, so the value of that money could be eroded by inflation.

INVESTMENT IN AGENCY SECURITIES

Agency securities are issued by agencies that are owned, backed or sponsored by the U.S. government. The most common agency securities are as follows:

GNMA – known as Ginnie Maes. GNMA securities are issued by the Government National Mortgage Association.

FNMA – known as Fannie Maes. FNMA securities are issued by the Federal National Mortgage Association.

FHLMC – known as Freddie Macs. FHLMC securities are issued by the Federal Home Loan Mortgage Corporation.

FHLB - These securities are issued by the Federal Home Loan Bank.

These sponsored agencies, as in the case of all investments, have both benefits and risks. The benefits include the stability of principal. Some agency securities are backed by the full faith and credit of the U.S. government while others carry less formal guarantees, but all are considered to have high credit qualities.

Disadvantages include the risk of prepayment. Prepayment risk is the possibility that, as interest rates fall, homeowners will refinance their mortgages. You, then, must reinvest this prepaid principal sooner than you had anticipated and possibly at a lower interest rate.

Additional risks include interest rate risk. The market value of your securities could decline due to rising interest rates. Then there's the risk of less current income. Because they have high credit quality, agency securities provide less interest income than bonds with comparable maturities and lower credit ratings.

Finally comes inflation risk. The interest income you earn from a bond investment remains the same over the life of the bond. The value of that money could be eroded by inflation.

INVESTMENT IN CORPORATE BONDS

Corporate bonds are debt instruments of varying credit quality issued in a range of maturities by corporations. Corporate bonds vary according to both credit quality and maturity or length of the term. Consider first the maturity variances. Corporate bonds range from short-term (less than 5 years) to intermediate-term (5–10 years) to long-term (more than 10 years).

Now let's take a look at the credit quality factor. Most corporate bonds are assigned a letter-coded rating by independent bond-rating agencies such as Moody's Investors Service, Inc. and Standard & Poor's Corporation. The rating indicates the likelihood that the issuer will pay interest and repay the principal in full and on time.

Bonds rated BAA or higher by Moody's or BBB or higher by Standard & Poor's are called investment-grade bonds. Bonds rated BA or lower by Moody's or BB or lower by Standard & Poor's are known as high-yield bonds (because of the higher interest rates they must pay to attract investors) or junk bonds (because of the possibility that the issuer will default).

When deciding whether or not to invest in corporate bonds, also consider the benefits of having current income. Corporate bonds generally provide higher interest income than Treasuries and agency bonds because they are considered to be less safe than government securities and the market rewards investors for assuming even a small amount of additional risk.

When considering whether or not to invest in corporate bonds, also consider the potential disadvantages. First, consider the possibility of a call risk. Again, during periods of falling interest rates, corporate bond issuers may prepay or call their loans before maturity in order to reissue the loans at a lower rate so that you as the lender must reinvest this pre-paid principal sooner than you had anticipated and possibly at a lower interest rate.

There is always a great possibility of credit risk. You could lose money if a bond issuer (corporation) defaults, that is, fails to make timely payments of principal and interest or a bond's credit rating is reduced. There is event risk as there would also be in buying equities.

The credit quality or market value of your bonds could suffer in response to an event such as a merger, leveraged buyout, or other corporate restructuring. There can be tax consequences. The interest income on your corporate bonds (unlike the interest income on treasuries and some agency securities) is taxable at the federal, state and local levels.

You also have to consider the interest rate risk. The market value of your bonds could decline due to rising interest rates. And finally there is the risk of inflation. The interest income you earn from a bond investment remains the same over the life of the bond. The value of that money could be eroded by inflation.

Investment in Municipal Bonds

Municipal bonds (often referred to as "munis") are issued by state and local governments to finance public projects or support other financial needs. These bonds are attractive to investors in higher tax brackets because their interest income generally is exempt from federal and state taxes.

Municipal bonds also known as tax-exempt or tax-free bonds are available in two main types. Revenue bonds are used to finance municipal projects that generate revenue (a toll road, for example). This revenue is used to make interest and principal payments to the bond holders.

Another municipal bond is classified as a general obligation bond. These are issued for municipal projects that do not generate revenue (such as a government office building). These bonds are backed by the full faith and credit of the issuer and are repaid with taxes assessed by the issuer.

Municipal bonds, like other bonds, can vary widely in credit quality and maturity. There are certain tax advantages when purchasing municipal bonds. You should consult your CPA for information about them. Disadvantages include less than current income, interest rate risk, call risk, credit risk and inflation risk.

INVESTMENT IN COMMON STOCKS

Common stocks represent part ownership or equity in a public corporation. Companies issue stock as a way to raise money to expand or build their business.

When you buy stock, you hope that the value of your investment will grow. Market value is determined by such factors as a company's current earnings and long-term growth prospects, overall trends in the securities markets, and economic conditions.

Many companies also distribute a portion of their profits to stock owners in the form of regular dividends. If a company encounters difficulties, however, the value of your investment could decline. The company could stop paying dividends or the market value of the stock could decrease. Because stock prices tend to fluctuate suddenly and sometimes sharply, stocks are considered riskier than bonds or cash investments.

The strong stock market of the 1990's lulled many investors into a false sense of security. If there's one thing you should know about stocks, it's that the stock market is unpredictable. The value of your stock could rise one day and decline the next. So, while stocks offer the potential for regular dividends and significant capital growth, they also present substantial risks.

Of course, there are many potential benefits to owning stocks. One is the possibility of long-term growth. Over the long haul, stocks tend to offer you the greatest potential return on your investment.

Since 1926, according to experts, common stocks have returned an average of 11.2 percent annually — more than bonds or cash investments and well ahead of inflation. There is also the potential for current income through stocks that pay regular dividends, which you can receive as cash or reinvest in more shares. Companies differ, however, in how much of their profits they distribute to shareholders and how much they put back into the company.

The long list of disadvantages begins with a huge one; market risk. The price of your stock could decline over short or even extended periods. Stock markets tend to move in cycles, with periods when prices rise and other periods when prices fall. (Price declines can be dramatic: On October 19, 1987, the Standard & Poor's® 500 Composite Stock Price Index fell 20 percent. And, in the worst bear market since World War II, the S&P 500 Index declined by 48 percent from January 1973 to October 1974.) In the years 2000, 2001 and 2002, the market had consecutive declining years.

Another very real consideration is the risk of losing your principal. You could lose money by investing in stocks. There is also industry risk. The price of your stock could decline due to developments affecting its company's industry.

And of course, as in many investment alternatives, there is event risk. The price of your stock could decline in response to an event such as a merger, leveraged buyout or other corporate restructuring. Because of their short-term volatility, stocks should be considered a long-term investment.

INVESTMENT IN MONEY MARKET FUNDS

Money market funds seek income, liquidity and a stable share price by investing in high-quality, short-term cash investments (that mature in 13 months or less), including certificates of deposit (CD's), Treasury bills, banker's acceptances and commercial paper.

Because cash investments are considered to be the safest of the three primary asset classes, these funds are ideal for stashing emergency money or cash that you plan to use in two years or less. Money market funds are low-risk investments that offer low returns in exchange for providing peace of mind.

The benefits of investing in money market funds include stability of principal. Cash investments are viewed as safe because your money generally is invested with reliable borrowers for only a brief period. In addition, the Securities and Exchange Commission requires that all taxable money market funds invest at least 95 percent of their assets in securities of the highest grade, as rated by Moody's Investors Service, Inc. or Standard & Poor's Corporation.

Of course there is the benefit of current income streams. Dividends, distributed monthly by the funds, typically are higher than the dividends paid by a bank savings account or CD. Another very good benefit is liquidity. Most of the funds offer free check-writing privileges and you can redeem your money at any time.

Disadvantages include inflation risk and income risk. Let's begin with inflation risk. Because cash investments are considered safe, the interest rates they pay are low and, over time, their returns have only slightly exceeded the rate of inflation.

From 1926 through most of the nineties, cash investments returned an average of 3.9 percent per year while inflation averaged 3.1 percent, leaving a return after inflation of only 0.8 percent per year.

Therefore, if you have a long-term time horizon, money market funds should not be your primary choice, although they can play a smaller role in a diversified investment portfolio. Last is income risk. Money market funds hold short-term investments that must be reinvested by the fund manager when they mature and possibly at a lower rate of return.

INVESTMENT IN BOND MUTUAL FUNDS

Bond mutual funds emphasize current income by investing in corporate, municipal, U.S. government debt obligations, or some combination. Bond funds can have average maturities that are short-term (less than 5 years), intermediate-term (5–10 years), or long-term (more than 10 years).

The primary types of bond funds are as follows:

U.S. Government Bond Funds. Invest in securities issued by the U.S. Treasury or agencies of the U.S. government.

Mortgage-Backed Securities Funds. Invest in securities representing pools of residential mortgages.

Corporate Bond Funds. Invest in the debt obligations of U.S. corporations.

Municipal Bond Funds. Invest in tax-exempt bonds issued by state and local governments.

There are many benefits in choosing bond mutual funds as a part of your overall investment portfolio:

✓ **Current Income:** While most individual bonds pay interest twice a year, most bond funds distribute interest monthly. You may choose to receive those distributions as cash or reinvest them in additional fund shares.

✓ **Diversification**: A bond fund may hold bonds from hundreds of different issuers, so a default by one bond issuer would have only a slight effect on your investment.

✓ **Stability**: In addition, because bond returns tend to fluctuate less sharply than stock returns, a bond fund could help reduce your portfolio's overall volatility.

✓ **Professional Management**: Few investors have the time or expertise to compare the thousands of bonds available. With a bond or stock fund, an experienced manager makes sure the fund's investments remain consistent with its investment objective—whether that's to track a market index or use research and market forecasts to actively select securities.

✓ **Liquidity**: You can buy or sell shares of a bond fund whenever you want. It's easy and there is no penalty for early withdrawal (although there may be a redemption fee, depending on the fund).

✓ **Convenience**: With most bond funds, you can buy and sell shares, change distribution options and obtain information by telephone, by mail or online.

There are, however, some specific disadvantages to be aware of with bond funds, compared with individual bonds.

• **Tax Consequences**: Unlike an individual bond, a bond fund has no fixed maturity date but maintains a rolling maturity by selling off older bonds and buying newer ones. These trades could create taxable capital gains (or losses) for you if you hold your shares in a taxable account. You could also realize a capital gain (or loss) if you sell your shares at a higher or lower price than you paid for them.

• **Income Fluctuation**: While your interest payments from an individual bond are fixed, income from a bond fund could fluctuate moderately as the fund buys and sells individual bonds. In addition, bond funds face the same risks as individual bonds, including interest rate risk, call risk, credit risk, income risk, inflation risk and event risk.

INVESTMENT IN STOCK MUTUAL FUNDS

The primary objective of nearly all common stock funds is to provide long-term capital growth. Some conservative stock funds may include dividend income as a secondary consideration. Stock funds (also known as equity funds) vary based on whether they invest in companies emphasizing capital growth or consistent dividends and on the market value of those companies (known as market capitalization).

There are three primary types of stock funds, which vary in investment style:

➤ **Growth Funds** invest in stocks of companies that have above-average growth potential.

➤ **Value Funds** invest in stocks of companies that are attractively priced; these companies frequently produce above-average dividend income.

➤ **Blend Funds** invest in both growth and value stocks.

There are also three categories of market capitalization (though a fund may hold stocks in multiple categories).

✓ **Small-Cap** invest in stocks of small, emerging companies (defined by Vanguard as having a total market value of less than $1 billion).

✓ **Mid-Cap** invest in stocks of medium-sized companies (market value of $1 billion to $12 billion).

✓ **Large-Cap** invest in stocks of large, established companies (market value of more than $12 billion).

Choosing to invest in stock mutual funds brings great potential to the table. The first is that of long-term growth. Over the long haul, stocks tend to offer you the greatest potential return on your investment. Remember, since 1926, common stocks have returned an average of 11.2 percent annually, more than bonds or cash investments and well ahead of inflation.

There is the very real benefit of diversification. A stock fund may invest in the stocks of hundreds of different companies. This helps to reduce your overall investment risk, because losses from some stocks are offset by gains from others. Mutual funds offer professional management. Few investors have the time or expertise to compare the thousands of stocks available.

Other benefits include convenience and dividend reinvestment. With most stock funds, you can buy and sell shares, change distribution options, and obtain information by telephone, by mail or online. Most stock funds allow you to reinvest dividends automatically in more fund shares.

And, of course, there are always a number of disadvantages to every investment alternative. Let's begin again with what is called market risk. Stock prices could decline over short or even extended periods. Stock markets tend to move in cycles with periods when prices rise and other periods when prices fall.

Then there is the disadvantage of investment style risk. If your fund's investment style is out of favor, its returns could trail the overall stock market or the returns of stock funds with different investment styles. For example, growth funds may do poorly when value funds do well and vice versa.

You can add to this management risk and principal risk. In an actively managed fund, poor stock selection by the investment adviser could cause your fund to lag comparable funds. You could lose money by investing in stock funds.

INVESTMENT IN BALANCED MUTUAL FUNDS

Balanced funds invest in a mix of stocks, bonds and cash investments. These funds provide a convenient way to achieve your desired asset allocation with a single investment. There are two basic types: Traditional balanced funds invest in a stable mix of assets (such as 60 percent common stocks and 40 percent corporate bonds) or maintain asset allocations that fall within a predetermined range (such as 60-70 percent stocks, 30-40 percent bonds).

The funds periodically rebalance their portfolios to maintain the desired asset mix. Asset allocation funds periodically shift their desired mix of assets in pursuit of maximum return when the market is strong and minimum risk when the market is down.

Traditional balanced funds are middle-of-the-road investments that seek growth, income and preservation of capital. Though they vary in asset allocation, a typical mix is 60 percent stocks and 40 percent bonds. Balanced funds offer the benefits of diversification in a single investment—with the accompanying risks of each asset class the funds hold.

The greatest benefit for the investor is that of diversification.

The greatest benefit for the investor is that of diversification. The fund enables you to create a diversified portfolio through a single investment. There is also less volatility. Because stock and bond prices don't move in lockstep, the price of a balanced fund is likely to fluctuate less widely than a fund holding stocks alone.

Balanced funds also enjoy potential tax advantages. The fund may be able to achieve periodic rebalancing by purchasing assets with money from new shareholders, instead of by selling assets, which could trigger a taxable capital gain. In contrast, if you hold stocks and bonds in separate funds, you might have to rebalance by selling shares of the fund in the better-performing asset class to buy more shares of the other fund.

Now it is time to consider the disadvantages. First comes market risk. The price of your fund's stock investments could decline over short or even extended periods. Stock markets tend to move in cycles, with periods when prices either rise or fall. With interest risk, the market value of your fund's bond investments could decline due to rising interest rates. And management risk occurs with poor stock or bond selection by the investment adviser.

CREATING A PORTFOLIO STRATEGY

There are numerous ways to allocate an investment portfolio. Every investment advisor has special favorites. The following represent a very basic opportunity to grow a portfolio over the long term within your personal choice of risk level.

Risk Level I: Preservation of Capital
20% Money Market Funds
20% High Quality Bonds
40% U.S. Treasury Bonds
10% Growth and Income Funds
10% Growth Funds

Risk Level II: Conservative Growth & Income
5% Money Market Funds
20% U.S. Treasury Bonds
40% Income Funds
25% Growth and Income Funds
10% Growth Funds

Risk Level III: Aggressive Growth
10% Money Market Funds
30% Income Funds
30% Growth and Income Funds
30% Aggressive Growth Funds

Principle Eight

Beyond Social Security

"Preparation for old age should begin not later than one's teens. A life which is empty of purpose until 65 will not suddenly become filled on retirement."

—*Dwight L. Moody (1837-1899),* Founder of the Northfield Schools, Moody Church, and Moody Bible Institute

Long-term Security Beyond Social Security

Financial security does not just happen. It takes a lot of planning, a heavy dose of commitment, and money. It is a fact, according to government statistics, that less than half of Americans have put aside money specifically for retirement. One third of those who have had 401(k) coverage available to them do not participate in the plan.

You can't retire with security unless you really prepare for it, and this means more than just Social Security Benefits. Long-term security requires us to live up to reality and to begin to take action for tomorrow as well as today. Putting away money for retirement is like giving yourself a raise. It's money that gives you freedom when you want it and when you deserve it.

Securing Your Retirement Future: Home Ownership

We should not begin a discussion about planning for retirement without first talking about home ownership. This is the first step toward securing your retirement future.

Buying a home is far more expensive than somebody who has never owned a home could possibly imagine. Too many people make the mistake of thinking that if they find a house with a mortgage payment equivalent to their rent payment, they'll come out ahead.

In reality, it can cost as much as 50 percent more per year in addition to the mortgage payment for expenses like insurance premiums, property taxes and maintenance. This does not include the money it will take to move, furnish and decorate.

Historically, in many areas of the country, housing has appreciated faster than inflation. Home ownership seems more difficult to afford. Many people think the biggest stumbling block to home ownership is qualifying for a mortgage. But far and away the greatest difficulty for most first-time homebuyers is accumulating enough money for the down payment and closing costs.

Although some lenders permit a low or zero percent down payment, it is much better to begin with an initial down payment of 10 to 20 percent of the cost of the house. A down payment is the difference between the purchase price and the mortgage that is taken out on the home. Closing costs can add another 5 percent or more, particularly if you will be required to pay points to the lender.

Points are an upfront fee charged by the mortgage lender. One point is equal to 1 percent of the principal amount of the loan. Points are also called loan origination fees.

Closing costs are expenses normally incurred by the buyer when purchasing real estate. They are typically 1-4 percent of the purchase price and may include fees for recording the deed and mortgage, escrow fees, attorney fees, title insurance, appraisal and inspection fees, and survey costs.

If you are tempted to resign yourself to a life of ever-increasing monthly rent payments, don't! It is possible to own your own home and it isn't as difficult as it may appear. By saving regularly and investing those savings wisely, you'll be that much closer to making the dream come true.

Planning for a House and a Home

There is no secret to saving. It's really just a matter of living beneath your means. Some people are very good at it, but many of us have difficulty saving regularly. Many prospective first-time homeowners are able to increase their rate of saving substantially once they set their minds to buying a house. The short-term sacrifice of foregoing some pleasant, but unnecessary luxuries, is certainly worth the long-term benefits of being a homeowner.

There is no secret to saving. It's really just a matter of living beneath your means.

The most painless way to save is to pay yourself first. Over time, you may be able to increase the amount you save each week or month, helping you reach your dream a little faster. You'll be surprised at how much you can save once your spending habits are under control.

As you are building your savings, you should also contact a few potential lenders to determine the size of mortgage you will qualify for. This will help you to estimate how much of a down payment you will need and it will give you an idea of the kind of home you will be able to qualify for.

Invest your savings wisely and avoid the temptation to choose those risky investments in hopes of reaping enormous gains quickly. Money earmarked for purchasing a home should be invested more conservatively, although you may be able to assume more risk if your home purchase is still several years away.

Appropriate investments may include U.S. Government securities, CDs, Zero Coupon Treasury bonds and low-risk mutual equity funds. A mutual fund is an investment that pools the funds of its shareholders in equities or securities. It offers participants more diversification, liquidity and professional management service than would normally be available to them as individuals and at a lower cost.

Mutual funds are often appropriate, because their diversification and professional management can lead to a greater peace of mind and less volatility than you could obtain by purchasing individual securities on your own. In addition, you can have interest and dividend income as well as capital gains automatically reinvested. This very convenient option may allow you to achieve even greater growth through compounding.

Home ownership has many economic as well as psychological benefits. Real estate has always been a solid investment, especially over the last few inflationary decades. If the value of your home increases, you benefit, not just your landlord.

There are tax advantages to home ownership as well. Interest on a first mortgage is deductible on your federal income tax return, as are property taxes. Within certain limits, interest on home equity loans is also deductible.

Buying a house at a relatively young age can be a potential help at retirement. More and more retirees are choosing to stay in their homes, which by retirement age are either paid off or have very low mortgage payments. They are able to use their retirement income to enjoy life rather than to make ever-increasing rent payments.

Other retired persons opt to sell their homes, thereby unlocking substantial equity that can be used to purchase a less expensive home outright or provide additional funds to assure a comfortable retirement.

A high monthly mortgage payment now may turn out to be a bargain in the future, because, as your earnings increase, your mortgage payment usually doesn't. If you doubt this, just ask someone who has owned a home for 20 years about their mortgage payments. Rent payments, however, will continue to grow each year with no end in sight.

Principle Nine

Planning for Retirement

I ncreasing numbers of people are finding that retirement is staring them in the face before they are ready to leave the work force. The job that they had counted on to sustain them in their later years may have been a victim of company layoffs. Many are facing employment which pays less and, more importantly, the loss of pension or retirement plans that they thought would be theirs. It is so important to invest personal money and adequately prepare for the golden years.

Retirement planning is taking on greater importance these days as more and more people face involuntary termination because of corporate downsizing and changes in the economy.

12 Considerations Before Approaching Retirement

The following 12 strategies can help you in the retirement planning process:

❧ 1. Know your retirement needs.

Retirement living is very expensive. How much are you saving for the future? Most financial planners recommend that you save 10 to 15 percent of your income. But many of us fall short of that goal. How much will you need to retire? How much will you need to save by the time you are 62, 65 or 66?

Experts estimate that you will need at least 70 percent of your pre-retirement income to maintain your current standard of living. If you are not making a moderately good living now, you may need as much as 90 percent of your current income in order to live comfortably in your retirement years. Just know that expecting Social Security to provide you with enough funds for retirement expenses is just wishful thinking.

᪢ 2. Know your future financial needs.

According to the government figures on aging, only one-third of the people now employed have attempted to learn how much they must save to achieve a comfortable retirement. Of those who have investigated it, still 42 percent remain unsure about how much money they will need to save in order to retire.

How much do you need to retire on? The answer to this depends on the lifestyle you foresee during retirement. It depends upon how long you live and how long your family members historically have lived.

The answer to this also depends upon your retirement goals. Do you plan to travel around the world? Do you plan to live just as you do now? How much money will you be passing on to your heirs? Some expenses will go down just because of your age. You won't be paying social security taxes, work expenses or contributing to retirement plans. However some expenses, like health care and travel may increase dramatically.

᪢ 3. Anticipate your future housing needs.

When it comes to living arrangements, most older people prefer to remain in their own home during their later years, even if it means some remodeling in order to accommodate their health concerns.

Even when frail and vulnerable or when afflicted with a chronic illness, people want to stay in familiar surroundings. This can mean hiring expensive health care professionals to come into their home to provide proper care. But often this is not possible when people have failed to save enough to meet such needs.

Adequate income and assets are critically important to enable-well being in virtually all dimensions of life in our later years.

☙ 4. Know your physical condition and potential needs.

A wealth of information is available on maintaining physical and mental health, as well as achieving an adequate level of economic security to remain as independent as possible. You can live an active life in retirement. You can lead a productive life and enjoy retirement.

The longevity of life in our day provides us with new opportunities for our retirement years. The aging of the population presents us with both new challenges and new opportunities. Of course, this also heaps more responsibility upon us right now to prepare for that lengthened span of life.

With long life becoming increasingly common, we realize that our retirement plans must address special needs that arise over a longer life span.

☙ 5. Learn about your employer's pension or profit-sharing plan.

Employment retirement plans are the most common sources of income that people have for retirement. Some employers still offer some form of retirement plans for their employees. These plans are an excellent way to invest money for retirement.

If your employer offers a plan, check to see what your benefits are. Find out about their plan and the details as to when and how you are vested. If you have changed jobs, go back to previous employers and ask whether or not you had any plan with them. Find out about any plans your spouse may have access to. Know what is available to you.

Also, you should know what vesting is. Vesting is a designated point at which you receive both employer's and employee's contributions if you need to leave the retirement plan due to a change in jobs. Once you are vested you receive both portions.

Prior to that point in your time of job service, you will only receive back from the retirement plan the amount of money that you personally contributed and you will lose the amount that your employer contributed. This is a very important factor to consider before you make any job change.

❧ 6. Contribute to a tax-sheltered savings plan.

If your company offers a tax sheltered savings plan, such as a 401(k), sign up and contribute all that you can. Maximize your contributions starting now. Your taxes will be lower, your company might kick in a greater amount to match your contributions, and you can probably begin with automatic deductions from your paycheck.

Over time, deferral of taxes and compounding on interest make a huge difference in the amount of money you will accumulate. For income during retirement, employees need to participate fully in these plans. If your employer matches your contribution to the plan, be sure to contribute as much as you possibly can.

If you change jobs and leave your current employer, consequently leaving your retirement plan, you may be able to roll over your retirement benefits into an IRA.

However, you'll need some good professional advice to avoid making errors in this transfer of your money. The check to transfer your retirement money should be made out directly to the IRA account, which is often referred to as a direct transfer. If the check is mistakenly made out to you, you run the risk of taxes and a penalty for early withdrawal, which may be deducted from the check.

❧ 7. Find out about your Social Security benefits.

Generally, employers are required to withhold Social Security taxes for their employees. This amounts to 7.65 percent from paychecks and contributes a matching 7.65 percent from the employee's income for Social Security. If you have been married for ten years, you may be entitled to a spousal benefit when reaching age 62. Check with the Social Security Administration for your eligibility to this benefit.

Social Security benefits are a foundation on which people can build a secure retirement. For most retired Americans, Social Security is the largest source of income and may serve to keep them out of poverty. Call or go online (http://www.ssa.gov/) to contact the Social Security Administration about your specific account. You can get all the numbers and estimated projections about your retirement benefits.

However, Social Security benefits were never meant to be the only source of retirement income. It needs to be supplemented with income from a company sponsored retirement plan, savings or income from other investments.

❧ 8. Put money into an IRA – Individual Retirement Account.

If you have earned income, you can set up an IRA. Earned income is the money you make from an employer or through self-employment. Unemployed spouses who do not work can also establish IRA's as long as their spouse has earned income. There are several IRA's, including traditional deductible IRA's, traditional non-deductible IRA's, education IRAs and Roth IRA's.

You can sock away thousands of dollars and delay paying taxes on the money until retirement with a traditional IRA. Or you can choose a Roth IRA, pay the taxes up front and not have to pay taxes at all on the accrued interest, dividends and appreciation when you retire.

The earlier you begin, the more you will have for retirement. If you begin at age 30 to put aside only $2000 each year, by the time you are only age 60, you will have an accumulation of $112,170 using a very conservative return on your investment of just 4 percent. As of this writing, you are eligible to contribute $4,000 each year, $5,000 if you are over the age of 50.

❧ 9. Protect your savings.

Don't be tempted to dip into your retirement savings. Not only will you lose your principal and future interest, you may also face stiff penalties and lose tax benefits. If you change jobs, roll over your retirement benefits directly into an IRA or into your new employer's retirement plan.

❧ 10. Follow basic investment principles.

How you save and put money aside for retirement is as important as what and how much you save. Inflation and the types of investment vehicles play a very important role in how much you will have accumulated at retirement.

Know how your funds are invested. Read books and understand what is going on with your money. Become knowledgeable. Trust yourself, instead of others for that final decision. Know what is going on in your financial world. Financial security and basic knowledge go hand in hand.

❧ 11. Remember the Rule of 72.

Let's take a minute to review the Rule of 72. This is an investing rule of thumb that calculates how long it takes to double your savings, given a certain rate of return. To use the rule, simply start with the number 72, then divide it by the rate of return that you expect to earn.

The result becomes your investment horizon or the number of years it takes you to double your savings. For example, if the interest rate that you earn is 7.2 percent, it would take you 120 months or ten years to double your money. You must be aware, however, that the Rule of 72 does not include adjustments for income taxes or inflation. The Rule of 72 also assumes that you compound your interest yearly.

❧ 12. Be informed!

When you don't know about some investment vehicles or you don't understand the process, get help! Ask questions! When kids are growing up, they continually bombard you with questions, sometimes to the point of driving you nuts! When it comes to financial knowledge, drive someone else nuts! Not just one person. Ask the same question to several different people, so you can be sure of the correct answer. Get advice, read books, gather information, take care of yourself.

Bring order to your financial world by being informed. There are many investment options and opportunities available to people today. Investment opportunities that help an individual plan for retirement include buying a personal home, setting aside funds in an Individual Retirement Account, and contributing to deferred income plans such as a 401(k).

The variety of investment opportunities makes the decision for proper investment of finances very complex if an individual is not willing to do his own homework and learn about proper investing himself. A CPA, a Financial Planner, or any other professional won't be of much help.

A person needs to trust only himself or herself when it comes to final investment decisions. Don't even trust your banker who wants to sell you CDs, mutual funds and annuities. Guess what? Your banker is a commissioned salesperson whose office happens to be at the bank! Just remember, no investments in equity issues are without risk.

5 MYTHS ABOUT RETIREMENT PLANNING

➤ Myth #1: "It's too early to plan for my retirement."

Whether you are close to retirement or many years away, it is never too early or too late to plan for retirement. You control your financial future by identifying your retirement needs, setting money aside and making wise investment decisions now. Tell some young family to start now to prepare for retirement and they stare in disbelief. They feel that they are still young and have lots of time before they need to save for retirement.

But the earlier a family starts, the more they will be able to salt away some great savings. That is because time is money and the power of compound interest is enormous. Assume you want to build a $100,000 nest egg by age 65 and that you can earn 10 percent on your money. You need to contribute only $16 per month if you start saving at age 25. If you wait till you're 35, you need to contribute $44 per month. The necessary contribution rises to $131 per month if you wait till 45 and skyrockets to $484 per month if you wait till 55.

Here is another example for you. Suppose you are a young person twenty years old. You start saving or investing just $21.40 each week and attain an average of 10 percent on your investment over a 45 year period. By the time you reach the retirement age of 65, your account would be worth $1,001,711.36. Over one million dollars! This shows you the power of investing just a little bit over the long haul.

On the other hand, some older couples excuse their lack of saving by thinking that they are too old to start saving for retirement. While it is very true that you can't make up for lost time and opportunity, it's never too late to start saving. Someone who takes early retirement at age 55 may still be going strong 30 years later. You'll have to contribute more to your retirement savings account than if you started it decades ago, but the time to start saving seriously is now.

➤ Myth #2: "I Don't Need a Specific Plan"

No one actively plans to fail in providing for a comfortable old age. They simply fail to plan. Our grandparents faced different problems with money than we do. They were frightened by bank failures and the depression and tended to put their money into just three places — a home, a bank and insurance. Today, we have to be prepared for the havoc that inflation can play on our investments over the long term, as well as corporate fraud or an up-and-down economy.

No one actively plans to fail in providing for a comfortable old age. They simply fail to plan.

Working men and women of all ages need to have a greater understanding of how to prepare for retirement. Increasing numbers of people are finding that retirement is staring them in the face before they're ready to leave the work force and that it's harder than ever to amass the nest egg they thought they'd have in their golden years. There are a number of common misunderstandings that could be dangerous to the future financial health of any working individual.

One common misunderstanding is that the conservation of principal should be a person's main priority. This is not always the case. Inflation is the deadliest money-killer over time and can result in a guaranteed loss of principal. It's not simply what you make on your money that counts; it's what you make over and above inflation that really matters. So your goal should be to conserve purchasing power, not just principal.

➤ Myth #3: "I'll be able to live on a lot less when I retire."

One real misunderstanding is that many people think that, upon retirement, they will be able to live on a lot less than they do now. While it is a nice little myth to tell oneself, it is hardly the truth. The only bills that will stop are your mortgage payments (only if you plan ahead for this to happen) and any educational costs you may now be paying. Your medical bills will almost certainly rise. Expect higher costs of food, fuel, clothing, transportation and insurance, too. This does not even include new taxes and upkeep on your home, even if it has been paid in full.

With the federal deficit continuing to balloon beyond our country's ability to finance its expenditures out of current receipts, higher taxes will be necessary to pay for the future health and retirement costs of our aging population. The only way you'll be in a lower tax bracket will be if you wind up living on a lot less money than you are today and that will mean you'll wind up in worse financial shape and be subjected to a more humble lifestyle.

➤ Myth #4: "Social Security is all I'll need."

Although Social Security benefits may indeed be there, don't put a lot of faith into the system if you are 40 years of age and younger. Even company pensions are rapidly disappearing. As the downsizing of businesses continues, many companies are closing their retirement plans or replacing them with less generous ones.

When the current generation of middle-aged workers retires, there probably won't be enough people left in the work force to fund Social Security benefits at the level to which today's retirees are accustomed.

Some people argue that living costs will be less because there will only be the two of them. Don't be too sure. These days, more and more adult children are moving back home because of economic setbacks or divorce. Many times the grandkids come with them.

The greatest service you can do for your kids is to raise them to be independent, to live within their means and to develop an appreciation for the value of hard work.

It is even common for children to go to college and then move back home. The result? More food to buy, more utilities to pay, etc. The greatest service you can do for your kids is to raise them to be independent, to live within their means and to develop an appreciation for the value of hard work.

➤ Myth #5: "I just need to live for the moment."

Some people seem to live only for the moment. They figure that, when they get old, someone will have to take care of them. Besides, they want to have fun now and enjoy life. They think that saving and investing will cramp their lifestyle. Well certainly it will cut back on the amount of cash flow available for fun things, but if a person will save just

10 percent of their current disposable income for retirement after taxes and tithing, they will still have 90 percent left for today.

An inability to live comfortably on 90 percent of your disposable income now means there is a problem with overspending. Saving and spending are not conflicting goals. Saving is merely not spending today so you can spend more tomorrow. And if you don't die young, you'll have plenty of time to savor the fruits of your frugality later on in retirement years.

Everyone needs a clearer vision of their retirement needs and the peace of mind that comes with knowing they are initiating an investment plan. Certainly, you should do a lot of reading from a variety of sources before making any kind of life-changing decisions.

A person needs to read and become familiar with their personal retirement needs as well as pinpoint their goals and identify investment strategies. This information is not designed to take the place of a tax advisor or financial planner, but is simply a means to help you begin thinking about how to approach the basic planning process.

THREE RETIREMENT QUESTIONS

▶ 1. "How much will I need for retirement?"

The basic rule of thumb used by many financial planners is that a person will need about 60-90 percent of their final income before retirement to maintain their lifestyle during the non-working years. Of course, this rule will vary with everyone's situation. But the best way to address this issue of expenses during retirement is to sit down and plan a budget.

To identify future expenses there are some key questions to consider. How much traveling do you want to do in retirement? Will your medical expenses and insurance costs increase once you leave your company? Will your mortgage expense change because you plan to sell your house and relocate?

After considering the kind of retirement expenses you will be faced with, consider next the income needed to cover these expenses. In doing so, be sure to consider inflation as a factor in your retirement planning.

Living expenses are likely to be greater in the future because inflation increases the cost of goods and services. It will require more dollars in the future to enjoy the comparable lifestyle you have today.

▶ 2. "How can I account for inflation in my planning?"

To address the issue of inflation, the easiest approach is to look at everything in today's dollars and then adjust income and return with an inflation factor.

For example, if you want to assume an average return on hypothetical investments of 7 percent and an average inflation factor over the years of 4 percent, then in your calculations, you would use a net 3 percent return (7 percent minus 4 percent). This approximates the inflation factor by placing all numbers in current dollars.

Do you know what a gallon of milk will cost in twenty years? How about a loaf of bread? The answer of course, we cannot know, but we do know that it will in fact cost more than today. Because of inflation, a dollar today will not be worth as much in the future.

Don't worry too much about inflation, because incomes generally keep up, more or less, with prices. The key is to plan for a retirement income which will keep you up with, or better still, ahead of inflation. If your after-tax return on savings and investments exceeds the inflation rate over the long run, you'll come out ahead and retain your purchasing power.

A simple formula for determining the investment return needed just to break even after taxes and inflation is to divide the current inflation rate by 100 minus your marginal tax bracket. You must exceed the result in order for your retirement savings to grow.

Let's say for example that inflation jumps to 5 percent and that you remain in the 15 percent tax bracket. Given this scenario the rate of return needed for you to breakeven is 5.9 percent. Should you be in the 28 percent tax bracket, your breakeven rate is 6.9 percent.

When it comes to investing, a realistic after-tax/after-inflation goal is around 1-4 percent above the breakeven rate. In the previous scenario, the 28 percent bracket investor should seek a taxable investment product yielding 8-11 percent.

Estimating income begins with the basics of most retirement savings plans. These basics include both Social Security, 401(k)'s and IRA's. Social Security provides only a base level of income.

You can affect the amount of your Social Security benefit by the age at which you decide to collect. Age 62 is the earliest you can collect. But if you begin collecting before age 65, your benefits will be reduced. And, if you delay until after age 65, benefits are increased.

Your Social Security benefit can also be reduced if your retirement earnings exceed a certain level of income while drawing Social Security.

▶ 3. "How will my retirement be funded?"

For many people, their own 401k's or IRA's will provide a major portion of retirement income. If you are fortunate enough to have a company pension plan, then all the better. A lot of pensions are provided in the form of an annuity (equal periodic payments over a lifetime), although some will give you the option to take a lump sum distribution at retirement. To identify your pension benefits, you should request an estimate of your expected annual pension from your Employee Benefits department.

Pension payouts during retirement depend on various factors, such as the length of time you stay at a company, whether or not a pension has an inflation adjustment, and your salary. Many people do not realize the impact frequent job changes may have on future retirement benefits.

RETIREMENT INVESTMENT PRODUCTS

Investment products for your retirement years should be chosen with your objectives, financial resources, and risk tolerance in mind. Another consideration is your marginal tax bracket. If you are in a higher tax bracket, you may earn a far greater return using tax-exempt investment products such as municipal bonds or bond mutual funds.

An additional important strategy in picking products for your retirement investments is to diversify your investments among several types of products. This reduces the risk of making a poor selection or other considerations beyond your control.

According to one investment firm (T. Rowe Price), a diversified portfolio (evenly divided among money market instruments, bonds, stocks and real estate) earned an average annual return of 12 percent between the years 1978 and 1987.

This was the result compared to no diversity returns of 15.3 percent for stocks during this same period, 13.5 percent for real estate, 9.7 percent for bonds and 9.4 percent for money market funds. Of course, over the past ten years these numbers have changed dramatically.

Diversification is the number one consideration for all portfolios. A well-balanced portfolio will, over time, produce greater yields more consistently than any one area alone. You will enjoy less risk, less volatility, more consistent yields, and less stress about the ups and downs of any one investment product or the nation's economy.

Retirement nest eggs can be accumulated through a number of investment possibilities reviewed below. To understand the investment options, see previous content discussed.

Tax-Advantaged Retirement Products

For anyone saving for the future, there are certain kinds of tax-advantaged products that must be emphasized for retirement savings. "Tax-advantaged" means that earnings will grow on a tax-deferred basis and in some cases you may also take a tax deduction when you initially invest. If you are saving for the future, the longer you can defer taxes, the larger your ultimate nest egg will be due to compounding.

Employer-Sponsored Retirement Plans

One of the simplest ways to set aside tax-deferred savings for your retirement is through an employer-sponsored retirement plan. Through automatic payroll deductions, the plans allow you to make voluntary contributions to the plan by setting aside part of your before-tax salary. Not only are the earnings tax-deferred until withdrawal, but the contributions reduce your taxable income.

Cash Equivalents/Money Markets

Basically, investments can be divided into four major groups, ranging from the more conservative to the more aggressive. Cash equivalents and money markets can be a conservative option for the investor. These are short-term, high-quality securities that pay dividend income with principal value remaining stable.

Income Investments

These are primarily taxable corporate and government bonds or tax-free bonds which can generate high, current dividend yields, but are subject to price fluctuations with interest rate changes.

GROWTH INVESTMENTS

Considered more aggressive, these funds typically invest in stocks with the objective of showing growth in assets over the long term. They have greater upside appreciation potential, but also present much more risk. Your particular retirement investment strategy will depend on a few personal choices.

What kind of risk are you willing to take? Are you a conservative, moderate or aggressive investor? How much time do you have until retirement? Are you close to retirement or many years away? What kind of investment vehicle are you interested in? Are you seeking income, growth or a combination of both?

ANNUITIES

These may be purchased as a single investment or a series of investments over a period of time. Earnings are tax-deferred until withdrawn and annuities may provide the additional guarantee of a stream of income over your lifetime. There is no limit on the amount you can invest.

MUTUAL FUNDS

Mutual funds are diversified portfolios of stocks, bonds or money market instruments. Managed by investment specialists, mutual funds are available with objectives to meet most levels of risk and investment strategies.

Since most investors should diversify their portfolios, mutual funds provide an easy way to buy shares in diversified pools of investment instruments…without having to purchase high-cost, individual securities.

Here are a couple of basic guidelines. The closer you are to retirement, the more conservative and income-oriented you should likely be. The longer you have until retirement, the more aggressive you may want to be in investing for long-term growth. This is because you have more time to ride out the ups and downs of the stock market.

SUMMARY

As I stated at the beginning, the purpose of this book was simply to give you enough information so that you can make your own wise financial investment decisions.

We started out by talking about finding the money to invest. Right away we noted that the secret to finding money to invest was to spend what you have left after saving, instead of saving what is left after your spending.

We urged you to recognize the risks involved in all investments and what you can do to minimize those risks. We also discussed common mistakes that lead to investment disaster.

After showing you several principles you needed to know about investing in mutual funds, we gave you some alternative investment options, along with their various advantages and disadvantages. Several ideas about retirement planning were also given to you.

But let me end with my beginning statement. Absolutely no attempt was made to influence you to invest in a specific type of financial instrument. Information was given to you that would help you, in just a few short pages, understand as much as possible about investments.

This should be the beginning, not the ending of your research and reading. Commit to spending one hour of each day preparing to make right investment decisions.

You can make it. You can be a successful investor. I believe in you!

Source Material

21 Unbreakable Laws of Success, Max Anders, Thomas Nelson, 1996

A Christian Guide to Prosperity; Fries & Taylor, California: Communications Research, 1984

A Look At Stewardship, Word Aflame Publications, 2001

American Savings Education Council (http://www.asec.org)

Anointed For Business, Ed Silvoso, Regal, 2002

Avoiding Common Financial Mistakes, Ron Blue, Navpress, 1991

Baker Encyclopedia of the Bible; Walter Elwell, Michigan: Baker Book House, 1988

Becoming The Best, Barry Popplewell, England: Gower Publishing Company Limited, 1988

Business Proverbs, Steve Marr, Fleming H. Revell, 2001

Cheapskate Monthly, Mary Hunt

Commentary on the Old Testament; Keil-Delitzsch, Michigan: Eerdmans Publishing, 1986

Crown Financial Ministries, various publications

Customers As Partners, Chip Bell, Texas: Berrett-Koehler Publishers, 1994

Cut Your Bills in Half; Pennsylvania: Rodale Press, Inc., 1989

Debt-Free Living, Larry Burkett, Dimensions, 2001

Die Broke, Stephen M. Pollan & Mark Levine, HarperBusiness, 1997

Double Your Profits, Bob Fifer, Virginia: Lincoln Hall Press, 1993

Eerdmans' Handbook to the Bible, Michigan: William B. Eerdmans Publishing Company, 1987

Eight Steps to Seven Figures, Charles B. Carlson, Double Day, 2000

Everyday Life in Bible Times; Washington DC: National Geographic Society, 1967

Financial Dominion, Norvel Hayes, Harrison House, 1986

Financial Freedom, Larry Burkett, Moody Press, 1991

Financial Freedom, Patrick Clements, VMI Publishers, 2003

Financial Peace, Dave Ramsey, Viking Press, 2003

Financial Self-Defense; Charles Givens, New York: Simon And Schuster, 1990

Flood Stage, Oral Roberts, 1981

Generous Living, Ron Blue, Zondervan, 1997

Get It All Done, Tony and Robbie Fanning, New York:Pennsylvania: Chilton Book, 1979

Getting Out of Debt, Howard Dayton, Tyndale House, 1986

Getting Out of Debt, Mary Stephenson, Fact Sheet 436, University of Maryland Cooperative Extension Service, 1988

Giving and Tithing, Larry Burkett, Moody Press, 1991

God's Plan For Giving, John MacArthur, Jr., Moody Press, 1985

God's Will is Prosperity, Gloria Copeland, Harrison House, 1978

Great People of the Bible and How They Lived; New York: Reader's Digest, 1974

How Others Can Help You Get Out of Debt; Esther M. Maddux, Circular 759-3,

How To Make A Business Plan That Works, Henderson, North Island Sound Limited, 1989

How To Manage Your Money, Larry Burkett, Moody Press, 1999

How to Personally Profit From the Laws of Success, Sterling Sill, NIFP, Inc., 1978

How to Plan for Your Retirement; New York: Corrigan & Kaufman, Longmeadow Press, 1985

Is God Your Source?, Oral Roberts, 1992

It's Not Luck, Eliyahu Goldratt, Great Barrington, MA: The North River Press, 1994

Jesus CEO, Laurie Beth Jones, Hyperion, 1995

John Avanzini Answers Your Questions About Biblical Economics, Harrison House, 1992

Living on Less and Liking It More, Maxine Hancock, Chicago, Illinois: Moody Press, 1976

Making It Happen; Charles Conn, New Jersey: Fleming H. Revell Company, 1981

Master Your Money Or It Will Master You, Arlo E. Moehlenpah, Doing Good Ministries, 1999

Master Your Money; Ron Blue, Tennessee: Thomas Nelson, Inc. 1986

Miracle of Seed Faith, Oral Roberts, 1970

Mississippi State University Extension Service

Money, Possessions, and Eternity, Randy Alcorn, Tyndale House, 2003

More Than Enough, David Ramsey, Penguin Putnam Inc, 2002

Moving the Hand of God, John Avanzini, Harrison House, 1990

Multiplication, Tommy Barnett, Creation House, 1997

NebFacts, Nebraska Cooperative Extension

New York Post

One Up On Wall Street; New York: Peter Lynch, Simon And Schuster, 1989

Personal Finances, Larry Burkett, Moody Press, 1991

Portable MBA in Finance and Accounting; Livingstone, Canada: John Wiley & Sons, Inc., 1992

Principle-Centered Leadership, Stephen R. Covey, New York: Summit Books, 1991

Principles of Financial Management, Kolb & DeMong, Texas: Business Publications, Inc., 1988

Rapid Debt Reduction Strategies, John Avanzini, HIS Publishing, 1990

Real Wealth, Wade Cook, Arizona: Regency Books, 1985

See You At The Top, Zig Ziglar, Louisianna: Pelican Publishing Company, 1977

Seed-Faith Commentary on the Holy Bible, Oral Roberts, Pinoak Publications, 1975

Sharkproof, Harvey Mackay, New York: HarperCollins Publishers, 1993

Smart Money, Ken and Daria Dolan, New York: Random House, Inc., 1988

Strong's Concordance, Tennessee: Crusade Bible Publishers, Inc.,

Success by Design, Peter Hirsch, Bethany House, 2002

Success is the Quality of your Journey, Jennifer James, New York: Newmarket Press, 1983

Swim with the Sharks Without Being Eaten Alive, Harvey Mackay, William Morrow , 1988

The Almighty and the Dollar; Jim McKeever, Oregon: Omega Publications, 1981

The Challenge, Robert Allen, New York: Simon And Schuster, 1987

The Family Financial Workbook, Larry Burkett, Moody Press, 2002

The Management Methods of Jesus, Bob Briner, Thomas Nelson, 1996

The Millionaire Next Door, Thomas Stanley & William Danko, Pocket Books, 1996

The Money Book for Kids, Nancy Burgeson, Troll Associates,1992

The Money Book for King's Kids; Harold E. Hill, New Jersey: Fleming H. Revell Company, 1984

The Seven Habits of Highly Effective People, Stephen Covey, New York: Simon And Schuster, 1989

The Wealthy Barber, David Chilton, California: Prima Publishing, 1991

Theological Wordbook of the Old Testament, Chicago, Illinois: Moody Press, 1981

Treasury of Courage and Confidence, Norman Vincent Peale, New York: Doubleday & Co., 1970

True Prosperity, Dick Iverson, Bible Temple Publishing, 1993

Trust God For Your Finances, Jack Hartman, Lamplight Publications, 1983

University of Georgia Cooperative Extension Service, 1985

Virginia Cooperative Extension

Webster's Unabridged Dictionary, Dorset & Baber, 1983

What Is an Entrepreneur; David Robinson, MA: Kogan Page Limited, 1990

Word Meanings in the New Testament, Ralph Earle, Michigan: Baker Book House, 1986

Word Pictures in the New Testament; Robertson, Michigan: Baker Book House, 1930

Word Studies in the New Testament; Vincent, New York: Charles Scribner's Sons, 1914

Worth

You Can Be Financially Free, George Fooshee, Jr., 1976, Fleming H. Revell Company.

Your Key to God's Bank, Rex Humbard, 1977

Your Money Counts, Howard, Dayton, Tyndale House, 1997

Your Money Management, MaryAnn Paynter, Circular 1271, University of Illinois Cooperative Extension Service, 1987.

Your Money Matters, Malcolm MacGregor, Bethany Fellowship, Inc., 1977

Your Road to Recovery, Oral Roberts, Oliver Nelson, 1986

COMMENTS ON SOURCES

Over the years I have collected bits and pieces of interesting material, written notes on sermons I've heard, jotted down comments on financial articles I've read, and gathered a lot of great information. It is unfortunate that I didn't record the sources of all of these notes in my earlier years. I gratefully extend my appreciation to the many writers, authors, teachers and pastors from whose articles and sermons I have gleaned much insight.

Rich Brott

ONLINE RESOURCES

American Savings Education Council (http://www.asec.org)

Bloomberg.com (http://www.bloomberg.com)

Bureau of the Public Debt Online (http://www.publicdebt.treas.gov)

BusinessWeek (http://www.businessweek.com)

Charles Schwab & Co., Inc. (http://www.schwab.com)

Consumer Federation of America (http://www.consumerfed.org)

Debt Advice.org (http://www.debtadvice.org)

Federal Reserve System (http://www.federalreserve.gov)

Fidelity Investments (http://www.fidelity.com)

Financial Planning Association (http://www.fpanet.org)

Forbes (www.forbes.com)

Fortune Magazine (http://www.fortune.com)

Generous Giving (http://www.generousgiving.org/)

Investing for Your Future (http://www.investing.rutgers.edu)

Kiplinger Magazine (http://www.kiplinger.com/)

Money Magazine (http://money.cnn.com)

MorningStar (http://www.morningstar.com)

MSN Money (http://moneycentral.msn.com)

Muriel Siebert (http://www.siebertnet.com)

National Center on Education and the Economy (http://www.ncee.org)

National Foundation for Credit Counseling (http://www.nfcc.org)

Quicken (http://www.quicken.com)

Smart Money (http://www.smartmoney.com)

Social Security Online (http://www.ssa.gov)

Standard & Poor's (http://www2.standardandpoors.com)

The Dollar Stretcher, Gary Foreman, (http://www.stretcher.com)

The Vanguard Group (http://flagship.vanguard.com)

U.S. Securities and Exchange Commission (http://www.sec.gov)

Yahoo! Finance (http://finance.yahoo.com)

Magazine Resources

Business Week

Consumer Reports

Forbes

Kiplinger's Personal Finance

Money

Smart Money

US News and World Report

NEWSPAPER RESOURCES

Barrons
Investors Business Daily
USA Today
Wall Street Journal
Washington Times

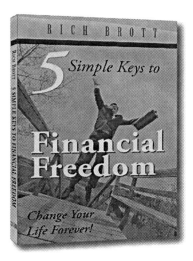

Additional Resources by Rich Brott

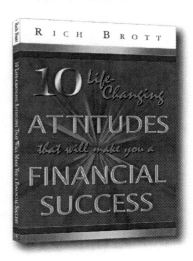

10 Life-Changing Attitudes That Will Make You a Financial Success

By Rich Brott

6" x 9", 108 pages
ISBN 1-60185-021-2
ISBN (EAN) 978-1-60185-021-8

Book Publishing

Order online at:

www.AbcBookPublishing.com

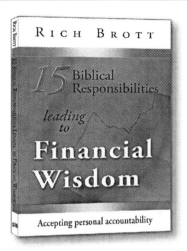

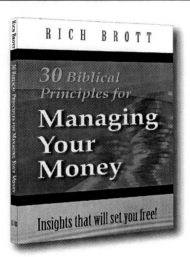

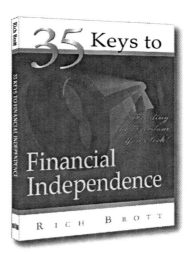

Additional Resources by Rich Brott

Basic Principles for Maximizing Your Personal Cash Flow

7 Steps to Financial Freedom!

By Rich Brott

6" x 9", 120 pages
ISBN 1-60185-019-0
ISBN (EAN) 978-1-60185-019-5

Book Publishing

Order online at:

www.amazon.com
www.barnesandnoble.com
www.booksamillion.com
www.citychristianpublishing.com
www.walmart.com

www.AbcBookPublishing.com

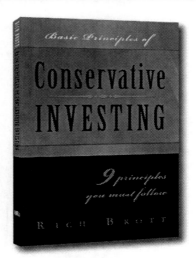

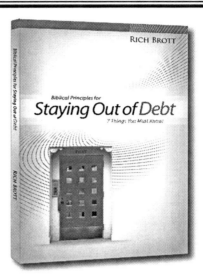

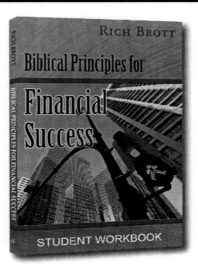

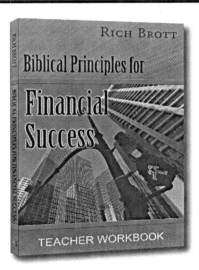

Biblical Principles for Financial Success

Teacher Workbook

By Rich Brott

7.5" x 9.25", 228 pages
ISBN 1-60185-015-8
ISBN (EAN) 978-1-60185-015-7

Book Publishing

Order online at:
www.amazon.com
www.barnesandnoble.com
www.booksamillion.com
www.citychristianpublishing.com
www.walmart.com

Additional Resources by Rich Brott

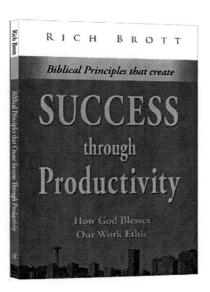

Biblical Principles that Create
Success through Productivity

How God Blesses Our Work Ethic

By Rich Brott

6" x 9", 224 pages
ISBN 1-60185-007-7
ISBN (EAN) 978-1-60185-007-2

Book Publishing

www.AbcBookPublishing.com

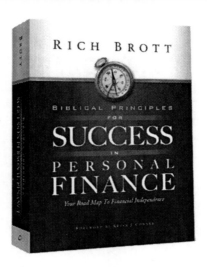

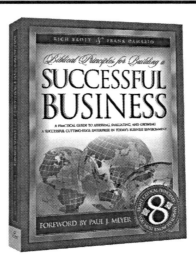

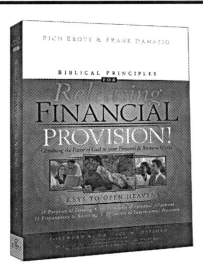

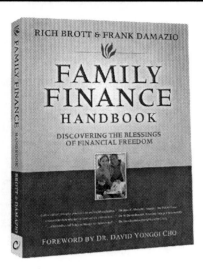

Printed in the United States
128041LV00002B/103-198/A

9 781601 850188